CW01635145

LONG DAYS IN THE HILLS

By the same author

INSIDE THE REAL LAKELAND
IN MOUNTAIN LAKELAND
PAGEANT OF LAKELAND
THE ROOF OF ENGLAND
STILL THE REAL LAKELAND

LONG DAYS IN THE HILLS

A. H. GRIFFIN

There is much comfort in high hills,
And a great easing of the heart.
We look upon them, and our nature fills
With loftier images from their life apart.
They set our feet on curves of freedom bent
To snap the circles of our discontent.

GEOFFREY WINTHROP YOUNG

Photographs by Geoffrey Berry and Dick Cook

ROBERT HALE & COMPANY

© *A. H. Griffin 1974*
First published in Great Britain 1974

ISBN 0 7091 4719 8

Robert Hale & Company
63 Old Brompton Road
London S.W.7

PRINTED IN GREAT BRITAIN BY
EBENEZER BAYLIS AND SON LIMITED
THE TRINITY PRESS, WORCESTER, AND LONDON

Contents

Illustrations

PICTURE CREDITS

Geoffrey Berry: 1–10, 13–15, 18–23, 29–40, 45, 46.
Dick Cook: 11, 12, 16, 17, 24–28, 41–44.

Acknowledgements

My thanks are first due to the many people who have accompanied me in the hills and on the crags—for their good company and, often, for their experience. And, especially on the many occasions when I have been alone, to the Ordnance Survey for their superb and beautiful maps.

Others who have helped particularly with this book are Stanley Bradshaw of Padiham who provided much useful data for Chapter 6, Geoffrey Berry of Kendal and Dick Cook of Bowness-on-Windermere whose splendid photographs illustrate the text, and my wife whose patience, typing and assistance with the proofs have been invaluable.

I would also like to thank Mrs Eleanor Young for giving me permission to use an extract from one of the fine mountain poems of her late husband, Geoffrey Winthrop Young, and to acknowledge that B. H. Humble's excellent book *The Cuillin of Skye* proved very helpful when I was writing Chapter 7.

The chapter end-pieces have been taken, as written, from my Lake District contributions to 'Country Diary' in *The Guardian*.

Cunswick End near Kendal A.H.G.
Christmas 1973

I

Mountains for all Ages

When Life Begins at Sixty

This is a book about mountain days on British hills, mostly in the Lake District and the Scottish Highlands, by a very ordinary mountaineer. No desperate ascents or hair's breadth escapes are recorded, although a few failures and mistakes are confessed. Rock-climbing is confined to a modest chapter or so for modern standards have soared too far, for detailed assessment, above my first adventures in nailed boots forty-five years ago. So that there is more steep grass and rough scrambling in the book than vertical rock and, even then, the author is careless enough, on more than one occasion, to get himself lost.

The book, however, may differ from other accounts of our homeland hills in that the emphasis, as the title suggests, is on rather strenuous days. There seemed no need to deal with walks up Helvellyn or Great Gable, but longer expeditions, embracing several hills, are increasingly being tackled today by those who wish to assess their fitness or prove some private point or just explore more of the district, and some of these are described. Years ago, we used to try to do six or more rock-climbs in the day, scurrying break-neck down easy gullies in between. Nowadays, some of us, not nearly so agile as we used to be nor so confident on steep rock, try to do at least half a dozen mountains at one go—and, if they are Munros, so much the better. The challenge, if you can call it that, is still there although muscle and co-ordination, especially the psychological factor, may be a little shaky. But I would prefer to call the impetus a spirit of adventure rather than a challenge. This is what mountaineering in all its forms, from simple hill-walking to Himalayan ascents, is all about—a search for beauty and adventure.

Another aspect of the book, which some people may find comforting, is that it has been written with the elderly mountaineer very much in mind. Being an elderly, and even decrepit, mountaineer myself I have a fellow-feeling for the aged but do not believe they should be mollycoddled—indeed, very much the reverse. Most of them could rise to heights never dreamed of, if they only tried. Perhaps these pages will encourage some of them to return to the hills again—or to discover them for the first time. They will discover that all is certainly not lost and that there is no reason, taking sensible precautions, why they cannot become freemen of the hills in their sixties or seventies.

Most of the long expeditions in this book—excepting the traverse of the Cuillin ridge which I did as a youngster of 48—were achieved when I was around 60 years of age or older. There is nothing in any way remarkable about this and I merely mention it here to place matters in their proper perspective. Indeed, so ordinary were these trips for a man in his sixties that I will probably never be forgiven by my friends for recalling them. In my circle there is no thought of giving up mountaineering just because one is drawing the old-age pension—rather the reverse. To finish one's professional or business career simply means, among all the mountain folk I know, that there is more time for the hills, and I could give dozens of examples of how this opportunity has been seized with both hands. But to underline my point, that you can carry on mountaineering to almost any age, if the interest is there, let me give four examples, all four friends of mine—at least until they read this book when I risk wholesale condemnation and scorn. One of them is Ivan Waller, who appears elsewhere in the book—a tough climber and skier who retired to the Lake District so that he could be handier to the mountains. In May 1931 he took part, with the legendary Colin Kirkus, in the first ascent of that magnificent climb Mickledore Grooves on Scafell. And forty-two years later, at the age of 66, he did the climb again, with a young and bold leader—just to prove to himself he could do it. He told me that on his second ascent he found the easy bits rather harder and the hard bits a little easier—whatever that may mean. Long after the national retiring age Ivan was climbing very severes and also doing a lot of walking. Not long after going round the Lakeland 'three thousands' with me he went round again, in bad weather—just for the fun of it. He also did the Haute route in the Alps on skis at an age when most people have long since given up the mountains.

Climbing with me on Dow Crag in 1973 was another friend, Eric Arnison of Penrith, then a very young-looking 72. Four years earlier he had become the oldest man to climb Mount Kenya and he is still climbing, skiing or fell-walking every week. Another mountain friend for forty years, Dick Cook of Windermere, completed all the Scottish Munros and the 3,000 feet tops—545 of them altogether—in 1973, at the age of 71—perhaps the oldest man to have achieved this feat. While when I was last talking to 'Rusty' Westmorland of Threlkeld—a genuine link with the climbing pioneers—he was planning, in his late eighties, his annual skiing trip to Norway. And 'Rusty' had not yet finished his climbing, which dates back to the end of last century. In view of all this it is difficult to understand climbers or walkers of 40, 50 or 60 years of age who say they are too old for the mountains. It is true that to rock-climb to a reasonable standard you have got to keep at the game fairly regularly; certainly it is true in my case. I returned to the crags in 1973 after a short absence and found, on a familiar cliff, that the holds seemed smaller and farther apart than on my last visit. There were also all sorts of awkward places I had never noticed before. Steepish rock, when you are not climbing regularly, gets steeper with neglect and I find that I need a succession of at least three or four weekends to feel even reasonably under control again. Regular mountain walking, as rough as possible with plenty of scrambling thrown in, keeps you fit enough—but not necessarily for rock-climbing, where you must immediately adjust to new psychological problems and be prepared to submit your body anew to long-neglected gymnastic postures. Confident stepping-up on small holds and off-balance moves come automatically to the regular weekend climber but, after a long absence from the rocks, the rhythm and the former neat elegance have to be discovered afresh.

But easier climbing, adjusted to the competence of the individual, and the whole freedom of the mountains, are there for the outdoor enthusiast, with a reasonably sound constitution, up to almost any age—particularly if he has been accustomed to the hills. So that this is one of the modest aims of the book—to encourage lovers of the open-air to continue their mountaineering and fell-walking as long as possible and to refuse to be tricked into believing they are too old for the job at 60—or any other age. And to fire their enthusiasm, although not expecting their emulation, I have included a chapter on record-breaking walks and runs in the mountains by the modern breed of superbly fit athletes who, perhaps not surprisingly, include a man in his sixties. It is not suggested that these extraordinary performances are within the grasp of ordinary folk, either old or young, but at least they show what is possible and give us some idea of what it must be like to be really fit.

Although most of the longer expeditions in this book were done at an age when many people are judged to be too old even for office work, there are also some nostalgic peeps into the past. Too much looking back is said to be a sign of increasing senility but may perhaps be excusable if the reminiscences are interesting. As I write, the country is in the middle of 'the worst crisis' since the war, with a bleak future ahead and millions of people uncertain about their jobs, their savings and the petrol for their cars. And all the heating and lighting in my house may well be switched off before I finish typing this page. Some of the most splendid wild areas in Britain risk ruin by wholesale commercialization and—if we ever get through the fuel crisis—other delectable corners may have to be closed to motorists because the motor car has become the menace of the beautiful places. On the hills, some places are being so worn away by boots that fellsides are having to be rebuilt, while elsewhere scientists are using feet-counters to establish whether or not the limit of human pressure has been reached. So that, in these depressing times, it is tempting to look back on days when we knew nearly all the people who climbed our crags by their christian names, when the walkers' Corridor Route up Scafell Pike had not been invented and there was no track over Glaramara, and when yours might be the only car—or motorcycle—parked at Dungeon Ghyll. There were no climbing huts, no mountain rescue teams, no voluntary wardens, no litter-bins and no caravan or camping sites that I can remember. There were no double-deck buses but four-in-hands went over the passes and there were trains to Keswick, Coniston and Lakeside. The hardest rock-climb in the Lake District at that time was Central Buttress on Scafell, and, for the walker, it was considered a notable feat to walk round the 3,000-footers in a day. At Christmas 1973 Professor George Sansom who took part in the first ascent of 'C.B.' in 1914 wrote to me, in his eighty-sixth year, of his 'very happy memories of Lakeland'. So perhaps my memories of the 1930s and earlier when the people who invented rock-climbing as a sport were still alive, when there were no conifers in Ennerdale, and the village of Mardale had not been drowned, may be excused.

Much of my mountain walking has been in bad weather—not because I like getting wet or cold but rather because when you are young you tend to go out no matter what the weather. What a tragedy, we used to think, to miss the chance of a day in the hills just because it's raining or snowing or the clouds are down. These were care-free, happy-go-lucky days, but there seemed to be an urgency about them, almost as if we sensed that war might come again and some of us might not return to the hills. Nowadays, with our mountain days numbered, we seek out good weather and clear skies, but forty years ago, with a lifetime of mountain adventure ahead, we could never afford to waste a day. At one time, although I am ashamed to confess it, some of us even thought we would waste a day by merely walking the hills instead of climbing the rocks. A proper sense of values was to come later. But I cannot now recall regretting a single day in the hills. Something has been won from even the days that, at the time, seemed the most miserable—indeed, in retrospect, these have often turned out the most memorable. It is the contrasts that matter—the mists suddenly torn aside on a day of storm and cloud to reveal sunlit peaks, the transition from rain and mist to sunshine and snow, the warmth of a hut after a blizzard, a hot bath or a fire for wet, frozen limbs, or the simple luxury of a concoction made from jam and snow in the hot, blinding glare of an alpine glacier. A squashed, damp sandwich washed down with wine bottoms from an old gourd would be an unappetizing meal at home but, eaten on the fellside, in the rain, behind a pile of rocks, it can be an enjoyable reviver.

Much of my mountain walking has also been alone which to the experienced mountaineer, is particularly rewarding. Tried companions are essential in climbing—except to the few—and can bring extra pleasure to the most mundane walk, but there are times when a man wants to be alone with his thoughts in the hills. Conversation, however pleasant, can interfere with enjoyment of the scene. I find that, as a general rule, I go faster and farther and see and discover more sights and experiences if I go alone, and the challenge, however slight, is there to be enjoyed. You can go where you please, as fast or as slow as you like, and abandon all your plans for a new idea that has just occurred to you at any moment. In this way, it seems to me, you can attain the freedom of the hills—especially if you are fairly fit and have an all-round mountaineering background.

But, in addition to a tale of long days in the hills this book is also, in its way, a love story. Why so many of us have such deep-seated affection for great areas of uplifted land, the largest monuments of nature, is difficult to explain. All of nature has its beauty, even level fields, but mountains, to many people, mean much more. Whether it is the beauty of their changing shapes and colours, the changing hours and the changing seasons, the memories of our adventures on the heights, or the permanence of mountains in a changing world, the hills mean more to us than anything else, except the closest human relationships. For thousands the hills represent a way of life and even the most down-to-earth among us must feel for mountains, at times, an almost spiritual attraction. In the darkest days of depression the hills can give a man new hope and determination. No matter what happens the hills will always be there to welcome us in their own way. Even to look at them from afar can be an inspiration to men marooned in lonely cities. How fortunate we are, those of us who discovered the hills in our youth and have had the good health to enjoy them for a lifetime. And how especially fortunate am I that I can see them every day, except when the mists are down, and that, in a very short time, I can be breathing the fresh air of the heights.

So many things are part of our mountain heritage—the speech of the dalesfolk, the old stone walls, the smell of the woodsmoke on an autumn evening, the wild life, the music of the becks, the silence of the woods and the cheery welcome of a country inn. There is so much more than the wind on the ridges and the challenge of steep rock, and sometimes you catch the spirit of the hills in strange ways and places. I remember once catching it, unmistakably, in the early 1930s when I sat in the drawing-room at the Wastwater Hotel—just after they had taken out the famous billiards table—and listened to George Basterfield working out the music, with one finger, on the piano, for one of his delightful 'Songs of a Cragsman' —'Eternal Hills'. Something about the scene—the kindly mountaineer, the famous inn that was the birthplace of climbing in Britain, the sad little tune, and the noise of the beck through the open window—persuaded an impressionable youngster that he had found

Innominate Tarn, Haystacks

Grisedale Tarn from Deepdale Hause

something that would last him all his life, And I remember, too, the sadness I used to feel in the old days when we came down from the crags or the hills in the evening. It cannot have been sadness at leaving the hills for we would be up there again the following weekend, and every weekend for as long as we liked. It must have been sadness for so much beauty that one just could not absorb, a feeling that nature had been almost too bountiful, that nothing really mattered except these wonderful hills, and that there was so much to see and to do and to enjoy. So I suppose I must have fallen in love with the hills in those far-off days and, although I have since discovered there are many other even more important things in life, I have been in love with them ever since.

A SUMMER EVENING

We came down from the crag in the evening with the long shadows slanting across the turf, the larks singing high above our heads and little black lambs jumping happily among the boulders. All day long a blue heat haze had hung over the fells but now, with the sun dipping behind the Scafells, the distant views were emerging into sharp focus, and the map coming to life below our feet like a photograph in a developing tank. Morecambe, 23 miles away as the raven flies, was easily identified and there, much further south across the bay, perhaps 30 miles away, we could make out Fleetwood. Somewhere near Lancaster the sun glinted on a car windscreen and high up on our fellside we caught the distant twinkle. Thirty-five miles across the fells reared, unmistakably, the flat top of Ingleborough and, much closer at hand, we could see the yellow line of the Flookburgh sands, the northern half of Walney Island and the tiny spike of the lighthouse monument on the Hoad at Ulverston. Almost at our feet, or so it seemed, lay the shining blue length of Coniston Water and the splendour of the picture was the blending of this splash of Mediterranean colour with the lighter blue of the sea, the green sunlit carpet of the fells and the richer shades of the crowded woodlands. Only a day or two before we were still in the wettest Lakeland May in memory, with nearly 13 inches of rain in Langdale but now, suddenly, it seemed the middle of summer and the most magical of evenings. The turf was springy to our feet as we trotted down the familiar fellside with the beck splashing its way down to the lake and, high up on the left, the ravens circling their lonely sanctuary above the dark tarn and the shadowed crag.

2

The Approach to the Hills

Some Suggestions and Advice

Mountain memories come winging easily back down the years at the sight of an old photograph, a dog-eared map, or perhaps a bit of rock picked up on some Alpine peak. Here is a yellowing picture of a small boy in school cap and shorts on top of Stickle Pike—my first summit—and here is the old red guide to Dow Crag, almost falling to pieces after forty-five years of rain and rough handling, with a scribbled list at the end of 'climbs possible with a 50-foot rope'. We only had a 50-foot rope in those days—half of a longer rope that had been cut in two by a falling rock and given to me by a senior climber who had taken pity on my improvidence. With this frayed lifeline we went slowly through the climbs, from the easiest to the most difficult, putting a little dot against the climbs we had done, with a circle round the dot when we had led the climb. I see that by 1930 I had managed to lead Central Chimney and Murray's Route but had merely been taken up Hopkinson's Crack on somebody else's rope.

But rock-climbing is only part of a full mountain life. To many of us it may be the most exciting and demanding part, a period in our mountain education when we test nerves and balance to a degree rarely required in other activities, but to taste the full flavour of mountains one must savour many other experiences from leisurely summer walks over the heights to winter climbs up snow and ice gullies, from ridge-walking to ski-mountaineering. We start by walking up easy mountains, graduate to rock-climbs and then, in our declining years—if we are fortunate—go back to the hills remembered from our youth. I remember Jim Cameron, the

Coniston guide who has done more climbing in his lifetime than most people, once telling me that, looking back, he had enjoyed fell-walking more than rock-climbing, and that the days he recalled most clearly were hill days in bad weather. After nearly half a century in the hills myself I would say he was right. To know a mountain really well, in all weathers, is probably more important than knowing a rock-climb, however difficult, for the climb is only one feature of the mountain. Looking back over a lifetime of mountains a hundred climbs seem to merge into one, although, years afterwards, one may be able to remember, for instance, the sequence of moves out of the cracks on to the face on Eagle's Nest, the trick of completing the first pitch of Eliminate C or the right hold for the finish of Asterisk. But I can remember with even greater clarity my first view of Dunnerdale in the evening sunlight from the top of Dow Crag in the late 1920s and recall nearly every yard of a scramble in the Skye hills perhaps forty years ago.

A shelf full of maps to most of the mountain areas of Britain, some of them so tattered and blurred that much of the printing is illegible, seem to stir the memories most easily. In a flash we are by the summit cairn on Scafell at midnight above a sea of cloud, or watching the sun peeping over Blaven at dawn from the Cuillin ridge, or struggling over the pinnacles of Liathach in a gale of wind and driving rain, or standing on the top of Bowfell with the mist suddenly torn away and the dale leaping up from far below our feet. Fifty years of mountains, a thousand bright mornings with the fells beckoning in the sunlight, and a thousand evenings when we have trotted down from the tops with the shadows lengthening across the turf and the sun dipping down behind purple hills. There have been other days, too—days of some danger on steep rock or icy ridges—but the overall memory is of friendly hills. The world is changing every day, getting smaller, more crowded; more ordered in some places where one would have preferred the former untidiness of natural beauty, and, in other places, dirtier, noisier and uglier. Only the hills remain unchanged.

The sheer scope of mountain potential in Britain, just the number of hills, is staggering enough. If you count every excrescence there are more than 200 fells in the Lake District alone that top the 2,000 feet contour—the total for England is said to work out at 349—while there are thousands in Scotland. (The 'Munros' have been counted and catalogued but I have never seen a total of the 2,000-

footers north of the Border.) Guide-books indicate routes of ascent up the popular mountains but the scope for the individualist, seeking his own way up and not necessarily the way that everybody else has gone, is immense. Even in the Lake District, which I see every day from my windows and where I have been wandering for a lifetime, I can still find new corners where I have never been before.

One day it was a different way on to High Raise out of Far Easdale, another time a delightful little hidden valley under Mellbreak, an unnamed tarn on Steel Fell, a rock traverse above Hardknott Pass or a 'new' way up Scafell Pike round the side of Esk Buttress. And, everywhere, scrambles up becks and waterfalls in out-of-the-way places, and rocky eyries, bilberry-carpeted shelves or thyme-scented belvederes where nobody goes except sheep. The opportunity for minor exploration, even in such a small area as the Lake District with the popular hills crowded with walkers every summer weekend, is still present. Go round the corner from a well-worn track or take a bee-line to a distant summit and you can be in 'new' country, while climbers are still not only working out new routes on well-known cliffs but even discovering 'new' crags. I can still find something new every time I go out, even though it may be no more than a different route off a familiar fell, a new view, at an unusual time of the day or from a strange angle, of a favourite crag or tarn, or just a striking cloud effect or an interesting flower. Indeed, when you've been up and down all the usual ways so often, you tend to eschew the popular tracks and seek out new ways, new corners, new experiences even though they may be no more exciting than an old cave below Pikes Crag or the discovery that there's a pool in the Liza deep enough for diving. The hills are different every day and there's always something new to be found. And it is to discover these new sights and experiences, dramatic or commonplace, that the connoisseur returns, over and over again, to the hills.

All sorts of people get into the hills nowadays, people who have never been on a mountain before, inexperienced youngsters seeking a new adventure and ordinary motor-car tourists, suddenly in hill country for the first time after a long motorway drive from the south. One autumn day in 1972 I met a lone walker on the ridge up to Hart Crag who had just driven up from London and was returning the next day. He wore a smart new anorak and carried a rucksack containing a flask of coffee, a flask of soup and, incongruously, a copy of *The Times*, but his footwear consisted of the low shoes he wore on the London streets or, more likely, judging from their appearance, a pair he had discarded. He was keen and fit and obviously enterprising—he intended to camp at Hartsop that night—but the descent from Cofa Pike almost tore his shoes to pieces and he finished the day limping back to his car. It was towards the end of one of the longest droughts I can remember in the Lake District and the fells were drier than I have ever known them. On an average Lakeland day his shoes would have been almost sucked off his feet; a week or two later, with ice on the rocks and snow on the fells, they could have been lethal.

Every year the sad catalogue of mountain accidents in the Lakeland hills lists people wearing Wellington boots or some other equally unsuitable footwear who have come to grief. Every winter inexperienced walkers—often young people ineffectively led by adults—slide out of control on steep hard snow, the fortunate escaping with bruises but a few falling over crags or down rocky gullies to their deaths. And, regularly, people are lost in the hills, the lucky ones being found, shaking and shivering, by rescue teams, but some succumbing to the insidious effects of exposure, the wet-cold that lowers resistance and can finally destroy the will to live.

The impression given to the general public by all these much-publicized searches, mishaps and tragedies is that the Lakeland hills are dangerous places to be avoided by sensible people. Here is an account of a string of schoolboys on a fell-walk. They are scrambling up a rocky gully when a loose boulder is dislodged and one boy is killed and others injured. And a few weeks later a middle-aged couple walking across the snow lose their footing and slide out of control down a gully, the wife falling to her death. These, and others like them, are terrible tragedies but it should not be concluded that there are perils round every corner in the hills or that one has to be lucky to emerge unscathed from the simmering wrath of the mountains. Most mountain folk, climbers and walkers, have never been injured or lost in the hills, although they have probably had their adventures, and very many people can look back on an accident-free lifetime of experience on the rocks and in the fells. Mountain climbing—except among those attempting the most difficult ascents—is probably safer than pleasure motoring.

And most of the tragedies and mishaps on British hills—the figures show that walkers are more prone to disaster or requiring rescue than climbers—could be avoided if only people had been better led, had studied the rules, or had had the proper clothing and equipment.

Mountain boots, warm and windproof clothing, a little food and map and compass are basic requirements for a day in the hills, no matter what the weather in the valley at the start of the walk or climb. In winter-time the requirements are more stringent, embracing extra clothing, and when there is a likelihood of snow or ice on the tops—sometimes unseen from the valley—an ice-axe should always be carried. Crampons (sets of spikes which are attached to the boots) are nowadays a necessity for winter mountaineering and their use by ordinary mountain walkers in winter-time would have prevented many serious accidents. There are several lightweight makes on the market that can be carried on the outside of the rucksack and only used when the need—crossing steep slopes of hard snow—arises. A whistle should also be carried for use in emergency and torches are sensible on short winter days.

Modern mountain boots have rubberized soles that are generally excellent for dry rock, grass, scree and soft snow, but these boots, especially when worn by the relatively inexperienced, can be potentially lethal on damp, lichenous rock, hard snow and ice. When I started rock-climbing in the late 1920s everybody wore nailed boots for climbing and walking, although rubber plimsolls were used for the hardest climbs. In the Lake District we mostly used fairly soft clinker edge-nails into which the harder rock would bite, giving a firm grip—tricouni nails were popular in Wales and other places—and this footgear seemed ideal for all but the most severe rock-climbing. However, on climbs where the holds were scraped and polished by much traffic you had to be very exact with the placing of your boots on the rock, keeping the lower leg at right angles to the holds and stepping up without allowing the boot to slide off. I remember one day paddling about in my clinker-shod 'iron boots' on an easy severe on Dow, which I had led many times, and making very heavy weather of it because the rock was greasy and I was off form. My companion was Jim Birkett, the Little Langdale quarryman who in his day was perhaps the best nailed-boot climber in England, and he took the opportunity to observe that footwear had nothing to do with climbing ability.

'It's the man inside the boots that counts,' he told me, to my dismay, after I had complained that my nails were worn. 'Just step up or we'll be here all night.' Perhaps I was demoralized by the fact that Jim happened to be wearing a pair of quarryman's boots with smooth 'caulkers', rather like those used on horse's hooves, round the flat of the soles, and no other nailing. In these he was stepping up with confidence on the tiniest of holds, whereas I would have felt unsafe in them on a rocky path.

But although Jim Birkett didn't think much of my nails technique that day in the 1940s I still believe that old-fashioned nailed boots—ideally, with waisted clinkers—are the best footgear for greasy or lichenous rock and also for hard snow and ice, if crampons are not worn. I still have a pair and wear them occasionally on bad days. They are excellent in dirty gullies and ideal for traversing rough, boulder-strewn country or descending sodden grass slopes. People seeing the boots regard me with amused and slightly pitying tolerance, assuming I have never heard of vibrams, but, wearing them I can get up greasy rocks in safety when far better climbers, in vibrams, have decided that the climbs are out of condition. One of my most terrifying experiences many years ago was leading a very distinguished lady climber up Tophet Bastion when the rocks were covered in a thin layer of slime. I was wearing vibram-type boots—they had not been on the market for long—and she, very properly, was shod in nails. The terror induced by my skating about on every hold was almost equalled by my shame in putting up such a miserable performance in such superior company, and my relief at reaching the top without mishap, but in appalling style, was profound. I don't expect, however, to be able to convince modern young climbers and mountain walkers about the excellence of 'iron boots'—and, of course, I admit that 'vibrams' have many advantages—but may I at least suggest that young mountaineers should realize the limitations of rubber-soled boots, and adapt their techniques accordingly.

Readers who have been co-operative enough to get this far must be told firmly, at this stage, that no matter what this book may turn out to be it will not be a treatise on technique and equipment, nor will it be a guide-book. There is an abundance of excellent publications handling these subjects and probably no need to add to them. What I will try to do is to convey something of the sheer joy to be won from the hills, particularly on long and sometimes fairly strenuous days, and also perhaps something of their challenge. To achieve this I must have my readers with me, either already captivated by mountains, which can embrace people no longer able to tread the hills as well as active climbers and walkers, or, having been stimulated by others, by books or perhaps an occasional visit, anxious to learn more about them. I have already offered a few general hints on footgear, clothing and equipment and, for the benefit of enthusiastic beginners only, will now attempt to give a few suggestions on how to get about the hills—how to walk, if you like. It should be clearly understood that I do not claim to be either an expert rock-climber or mountain walker or ever to have been one. Indeed, my friends will point to many occasions when I have dithered about on the easiest climbs or staggered, with irritating slowness, along quite short walks, but at least I can claim to have been climbing and walking for quite a long time, to be unlikely to fall and if lost—which happens on occasions—to be able to sort things out without calling out the rescue teams. I have also been lucky enough to have been involved in a few, undistinguished, first ascents and to have completed, after much toil, one or two fairly long walks. So with this rather shaky and possibly unconvincing background I will now come down to the basic business of how to walk. Later I will write briefly of rock-climbing but not so much how to do it—you can read the experts for this—but rather how to enjoy it.

Now, to get down to walking. It is perhaps a good idea to know where you are going although I must confess that I rarely do. When you have been up every mountain in the Lake District, and most of them by a variety of routes, you tend to be influenced by the whim of the moment—the sun shining on a particular shoulder of fell, the thought that it's a long time since you last had a look at Gable Crag or the Eskdale side of Scafell or the memory of a pleasant inn at, say, Threlkeld, which might provide an enjoyable finish to the day. True, one might have a particular walk in mind—getting the High Street ridge from Pooley Bridge to Troutbeck, for instance, out of your system, or working out an interesting rock route out of Mosedale to the top of Red Pike—but in my case it is often a case of driving north-west from my house and hoping the inspiration will come before I have driven too far. And it always does although it may sometimes be triggered off by something of no greater significance than the thought that on the very hottest day the water in Hard Tarn, under the Helvellyn ridge, is always icy cold.

This casual approach will, of course, be deplored by those who affirm that you should never set out for the hills without leaving behind a note of your intended route so that if you come to grief you can be rescued without unnecessary trouble. This is a good rule for the inexperienced and for the winter mountaineer or walker who must be aware of the much shorter hours of daylight, but I find it irritatingly restrictive. To have to go over Great Gable, your advertised route, when on reaching Sty Head you not only find the way crowded with ascending processions but also suddenly think of the counter-attractions of Piers Gill and a likely looking scramble up Scafell Pike by way of the side of Broad Crag, seems unnecessarily frustrating. I prefer to allow the day's adventuring to unfold naturally and like to be free to explore where I choose, as the mood takes me. To be forced to act otherwise would, for me, destroy the tiny spark of adventure that I believe can still be found in mountain wandering—even in such a thoroughly explored and catalogued area as the Lake District. But this is a purely personal approach and certainly not to be commended to all and sundry. By all means, leave word of where you are going and what time you expect to get down. And I will continue to tell my wife where I am going on solitary skiing or winter mountaineering expeditions—which I am sure should be condemned—but will normally leave the likely route of my summer peregrinations undisclosed, because I rarely know what they will be.

The disciplined mountain walker, however, will normally know where he is going and sets off, perhaps, from the valley in bright sunshine with the promise of a perfect day ahead. He should, however, be aware that despite weather forecasts assuring him, perhaps, of cloudless skies, almost anything at all, short of heavy snow in high summer, should be anticipated in the hills. It has, indeed, been occasionally suggested that the exact opposite of what the television weather experts have forecasted should be expected on the tops and you should at least prepare for this eventuality. Forecasted perfect days in the north-west can turn out to be miserably wet and cloudy on Scafell or Helvellyn and, equally likely, days when you are warned of heavy rain and gale-force winds can turn out calm, sunny and cloudless in the mountains. I had my most exciting day of thunder and lightning, with hailstones as big as marbles and a record downpour, during a traverse of the Coniston fells one summer when a perfect day had been forecast and after I had passed a party bathing in Church Beck.

The mountain walker, therefore, carries protective and warm clothing in his rucksack, no matter what the weather and at all seasons, as well as map and compass, food, and, particularly on the shorter days, a torch, together with other possible requirements, listed earlier. He carries the weight as high on his back as possible, not just above his waist, and in time he will be able to forget about it. Except on the very coldest days much of his clothing will be in his rucksack at the start. Walking up mountains can be very warm work, even in winter, and if you are accustomed to perspire freely, as I do, you will find it more comfortable to wear a minimum of clothing during the ascent. Whether or not it is a good or bad thing to exude so much moisture from the skin I have never been able to find out, but I am quite capable of perspiring when I feel cold, and on a warm day can lard the ground with a continuous succession of drops and be almost blinded with the salt from the perspiration dropping into my eyes. General Bruce who led the early expeditions to Everest had extraordinary perspiratory powers and once claimed that a minor ambition was to achieve a state when the drops off the end of his nose became a continuous stream, but that, regrettably, he had never quite attained this objective. Nor have I, but I must have been very near it on several occasions, one of these being an ascent of Grains Gill during a heatwave which was just like being in an oven set at about medium heat. I remember that, to cool off, we went up Central Gully on Great End—kicking our way up a bank of hard-packed snow, although it was June and the hottest day so far that year.

Because of the readiness with which my pores seem to work, I strip off to the waist on every possible occasion in the hills, especially when walking uphill, preferring to have a dry shirt in my sack for changing into later when I meet the cool wind on the tops. I commend this plan to other sufferers, adding the rider that it is most important to get dressed quickly when you encounter cooling breezes. Wind is one of the most insidious dangers on the tops and to get chilled after profusely perspiring can have serious effects. On a warm day it is also comfortable to keep one's lower limbs as cool as possible. I have never been an advocate of shorts for mountain walking, simply because my 'walking' can often progress into scrambling or climbing when knees are sometimes better covered, and because shorts can only be justified on sunny, summer days which occur comparatively infrequently. It is, however, a good plan to roll down socks or stockings and roll up breeches or trousers on occasions.

The cagoule is an article of mountain wear that I regard with mixed feelings. As an outer windbreak on cold, dry days or as a bivouac covering it is excellent, but as a waterproof, particularly on warm days, it has many disadvantages. When newly proofed—and the proofing does not last long—it certainly excludes rain but, as if to balance things out, encourages excessive perspiration so that you are soon fairly wet anyway. Another disadvantage is that the rain streams off the cagoule on to your knees, unless it is excessively long when you trip up in it. I have sometimes tried to turn up the lower edges of the garment to form channels to contain the water which can then be released as required, but this is finicky and not very successful. At one time I used to strip to the waist in rain using a cagoule as the only covering, but after a while found that I got unpleasantly sticky and wet. A reasonable alternative seems to be to put shirt and vest in the rucksack, thus keeping them dry, and to wear the cagoule over a thin sweater only. The sweater gets damp with the perspiration but you keep fairly dry and when the rain stops the wind or sun will soon dry out the sweater. Another alternative that I have sometimes employed in summer is to put everything in the rucksack when the rain starts, trudging along bare to the waist. This may look peculiar but, on a warm day and especially with waterproof trousers, can be curiously comfortable and refreshing. When the rain stops your body dries out in a minute or two, and all the clothes in your rucksack are dry.

For comfort, two pairs of socks are normal wear, the outer sock turned down over the boot-tops to help to keep out the small scree, while, in winter-time, some form of gaiters is required to keep snow out of boots. Boots are tightly laced for rock-climbing but on the approach to the crag or for ordinary mountain walking they may be rather slacker. It is essential, however, for mountain-walking—and especially when trotting downhill—that the foot does not slide forward in the boot, causing discomfort or even damage to the toes. For this reason I often lace my boots as tight as possible up to the instep, securing this section with a knot, and then finish off the top few fastenings rather more loosely, thus leaving a little more freedom for the ankles. Other people, however, may want more support round the ankles and have their boots tight all the way up, and sorbo-rubber can ease the chafing that this may cause. Walkers will find that boots can be tightened up considerably after the first hour when the feet have become bedded-in.

The mark of a good mountain walker is a slow, steady tread. The actual speed depends on the fitness of the individual, but to set off too quickly at the start of a fairly long day is a mistake. The great thing is to achieve a steady rhythm, altering the length of the stride to cope with the difficulty of the terrain rather than altering its frequency. In this way long distances uphill can be covered with little strain and few rests. Some people favour a rest of five minutes or so every hour, but when you are in fair training, this will not be found necessary. Stopping and starting destroys the rhythm. I stop to look at a view, to take a photograph or to eat some food—but never because I've been walking for an hour or two hours—and it seems a good plan to try and arrange for one stop to embrace a number of reasons. If you keep a steady pace and a good rhythm three hours without a stop may not be too long and by then most of the hard work of the day may be over. I find the first hour of the day the most tiring, even when I am in good training, and so I generally take it quite slowly and steadily. After that I may go more quickly. Many beginners find it more tiring to go downhill than up, which probably means that their thigh muscles are not yet working properly. On the ascent, no matter how steep the slope, every effort should be made to place the boots flat on the ground, instead of stepping up on the toes which is very tiring indeed. This ability to place the heel on the ground at every step should be conscientiously developed for it is very important. Alpine guides, who spend much of their time walking up very steep tracks, have the facility to an extraordinary degree and, with practice, it can be acquired by most fairly fit people. And the art is certainly needed in snow and ice climbing, wearing crampons.

Watch a Lakeland shepherd going uphill. He progresses in a sort of a roll, swinging his boots forward and turning his thighs to lengthen his stride. He is using the weight of his boots as an asset, instead of a hindrance, and this rolling movement, swinging the hips, is also worth acquiring. On the descent the knees should be kept 'slack', the heels dug well in, and the body leaned forward.

In this way steep slopes can be descended at the trot with great ease and speed, but proficiency only comes with considerable practice. Scree slopes provide a welcome means of descent if the scree is fairly small and runs easily. You really ride, in almost skiing fashion, on the moving scree, lifting the feet in long, low strides and jumping from side to side when the roughness of the ground requires it. 'Skiing turns' can also be devised when the conditions are right, but unfortunately many of the best Lake District scree runs are now getting worked out, and considerable care is needed when the scree has been swept off the surface, as on the Dore Head screes in Mosedale which, forty years ago, were superb. Novices should keep off screes altogether, until they know how to handle them. There have been several bad accidents on the Pike o' Stickle screes in Langdale, which is not a suitable scree-running slope, anyway.

A word or two about the use of map and compass. This is not a technical book so that I will leave readers to study the science of compass work in the many publications dealing specifically with the subject. However, it should be emphasized that the proper use of map and compass in the hills is not only a basic requirement, but a most fascinating study. Much of the joy of mountaineering and exploration, both in our low British hills and among the great mountains abroad, lies in the use of maps—in planning beforehand, on the mountain, and in pleasant retrospect afterwards. Men marooned in cities far from the hills relive their mountain days by turning out their old maps, and to plan forthcoming expeditions on the map, whether it is a round of the Wasdale hills, an Alpine ski tour, or a trip to Norway or the Himalayas, is one of the most rewarding aspects of armchair mountaineering.

In the hills, especially in unfamiliar country, the map will be constantly consulted to prove the route and to identify the surrounding peaks. The most important point is to know exactly where you are, on the map, at any time. This means that if you are overtaken by mist you can take a compass bearing of the next leg of the route planned, or, if the conditions warrant a retreat, the correct bearing of the route back to base. In planning a circular or triangular route it is often a good plan, particularly if bad weather may be expected, to work out the necessary compass bearings in advance, together with the approximate distances in between. Precise compass work, making the necessary allowances for magnetic variation, is a wonderfully rewarding art, which is not learned overnight and needs constant practice. The reward lies in hitting off a top or a track intersection at exactly the right place in thick mist or cloud, and in the knowledge that you can find your way home without hesitation. My advice is always to trust the compass even if the wind on your cheek or the lie of the ground persuades you that it is wrong. The direction of the wind can change quickly and the ground can look confusingly different in mist. These are, however, exceptions to this rule where the compass is unreliable, examples being the Bowfell area in Lakeland and the Cuillin ridge in Skye. During temporary clearings of mist it is always wise to recheck map and compass and confirm your position by a study of the view before the mists close in again. This is the basic reality of map and compass work—always to be sure where you are on the map.

The mountain-walker, especially if he is a novice and particularly in winter-time, should aim to get down before dark. Inexperienced people who press on to reach their chosen objective, disregarding shortened winter days, risk benightment, possible injury in the darkness, or the call-out of rescue teams. This last—unless occasioned by an unavoidable accident, which is rare—should be regarded as a disgrace, and not a slightly funny escapade which is sometimes the reaction of the rescued. One winter's afternoon recently I set off from Grisedale to walk over Striding Edge on to Helvellyn, a walk I have done dozens of times. I had just time to get up and down in daylight, moving fairly quickly, but on the Edge I met new snow and quite a lot of ice which, although I had an ice-axe, slowed me down more than I had expected. By the time I had reached the final slope to the summit the clouds had come down, it had started to snow and darkness was drawing in. Although I had a torch it seemed sensible to turn back for nothing was to be gained by scrambling about in the darkness. So I set off back down the Edge. About half-way down the rocky pinnacles I met a party of young people walking up. They had no ice-axes, one was wearing Wellington boots and the others town shoes or unsuitable suede boots. As I passed one of them was helping another—a girl—round an awkward corner. They were obviously having trouble with the ice and appeared to be completely inexperienced. The leader asked: 'Is this the way to Helvellyn?' and when I told him it was, he wanted to know how long it would take them. I asked him in turn whether he realized it would be dark in twenty minutes and whether they had torches, and advised them to turn back. He assured me that they would be all right and that they knew what they were doing, and when I repeated my advice for them to turn back he countered in rather abusive fashion: 'We've been up mountains before, you know.' Everything about them—their complete lack of suitable equipment, their ineptitude on the ice, and their disregard of approaching darkness—convinced me that their experience was minimal and their mountain manners inexcusable, but I was not prepared to argue further and left them to it. I hurried along the Edge, noticed that ice had formed below the wall since my ascent, and then trotted down the familiar track to my car at a good speed, the last ten minutes or so in darkness. Anxious about the party, despite their rudeness, I waited at Grisedale for about half an hour, the darkness now complete, but I saw no lights coming down the fell, and I don't suppose they had any anyway. There were no reports the next day of mountain rescue teams being called out so they must have got down all right, but at what time, and whether they got their summit, I don't know. The point of the story is that this succession of mistakes—bad equipment, bad judgement and lack of experience—is exactly what causes accidents in the fells, dozens of them every year. These foolish young people were lucky. I hope they had a fright and that they have learned some lessons.

Sustenance in the fells might be mentioned briefly, although this is largely a matter of personal choice. It is wise always to have some food in the rucksack for, although we nearly all eat too much and will come to no harm whatever if we abstain on a six hours' outing, there are times when reserve rations may be needed. Exposure brought about by cold and wet is the principal danger if marooned on the fells in bad weather, but lack of proper food can also be serious on long and trying expeditions. My father always took Bovril sandwiches on the fells although I could never stomach them, while one of my friends generally carries long, thin, black German sausages of a particularly repellent type in his rucksack. Another, believing that meat is the answer, relies on strips of beefsteak which he chews, with annoying persistence, every hour or so. The late Eric Beard, one of the most formidable mountain walkers this country has ever produced, used to get round his long expeditions, such as fifty-four Lakeland peaks within twenty-four

The Dodds from the north

Froswick from Ill Bell

Dale Head from Eel Crags

hours, on 'jam butties', while Howard Somervell of Everest who did the second traverse of the Cuillin Ridge in Skye reckoned he could have knocked an hour off his time if he had had a pound of raisins with him.

Great wads of food are not necessary on the average walking or climbing expedition. When two of us did the Cuillin Ridge in 1959 we left most of the food we had been carrying over the peaks for hours on Bruach na Frithe for the birds; we just didn't feel like eating. Similarly, over the years I must have deposited a considerable amount of unwanted food on various Swiss and Austrian mountains—although not, I hasten to add, in its packages—since much of the mountain fare provided in Alpine hotels and huts for climbers and skiers is either uneatable or unappetizing. Forty years ago one climbing friend of mine always carried great stacks of assorted food, done up in separate packages, each one correctly labelled and tied with string. He seemed to be overdoing things a little, but since, even in those distant days, he also carried every possible precaution against inclement weather, including heavy over-trousers and a complete change of clothing, you can see that he took his mountains rather seriously. My preference in those days was for jam or honey sandwiches and, as a second course, cheese or meat sandwiches, but for many years now my choice has been rather simpler. In winter I still generally take cheese sandwiches—meat now being too expensive—together with a few biscuits, but in summer I make do with a bag of raisins and some fruit. But, summer or winter, there always reposes at the bottom of the rucksack a little plastic bag containing chocolate, glucose, some boiled sweets, salt tablets and a few odds and ends—my emergency rations.

Bread, with fairly solid food in between, is not always appetizing in the hills, particularly when it is wet and stodgy and you are crouching behind a rock with the rain trickling down your back and your boots full of water. You feel you want something sweet rather than filling, and sometimes jam or even marmalade can make the bread go down easier—if you must have bread. Raisins are excellent for energy, sweet and refreshing and easily carried. (At the moment of writing there is said to be a world shortage of them, for some reason, and sultanas, for me, make a poor substitute.) Dates also make good food for the fells. Oranges or grapefruit are excellent on the mountains in summer-time, but the skins should be carried home in the rucksack, for they are remarkably impervious to weather and, if thrown away, remain for a long time as mute reminders that thoughtless people have passed that way. Banana skins, however, although not encasing so succulent a fruit, may be thrown away or hidden almost with impunity, for they rot very quickly, disintegrating within hours into shrivelled black strips which soon disappear altogether. Sometimes, therefore, I take bananas on the fells having been assured by no less an authority than the National Trust that their skins, unlike orange peel, are not looked upon with disfavour on their properties. Indeed, I once conducted a short campaign for the Trust trying to persuade mountain people to eat bananas instead of oranges but I don't think it was very successful and, in any case, my heart was hardly in the project for as a mountain delicacy on a hot day, a banana falls a long way short of an orange or, better still, a grapefruit.

On the question of drink on the hills my own preferences are simple—hot coffee or hot soup carried in flasks in the rucksack in winter and water from the becks in summer. It used to be said that you should abstain from drinking water on the fells, as trail hounds are taught to do, but I have never understood why this should be. Certainly, it is a good thing not to drink downstream of a dead sheep decomposing in the beck—although we once did this at the foot of Intermediate Gully on Dow Crag without any ill-effects—but there is nothing more refreshing than cool water from a mountain spring or stream on a hot day. I drink on the fells when I feel I want a drink not when I feel I ought to have one—unless I know there will be no water for several hours—and I think one's body is a good guide. Occasionally, when the sweat is streaming into my eyes, I take salt with it, against cramp.

Alcohol, for a variety of reasons, is in my view best consumed on the return to the valley and not on the hills, although it is apparent from the thousands of canned beer opening rings that litter the fells nowadays that there are many people who do not agree with me. This is not to say that I have not been greatly cheered on a number of occasions by the production, on some hard-won summit or climb, of a friend's gourd containing some infamous mixture of wines and spirits, with perhaps sugar added. Such a drink, particularly if unexpected, can raise morale a hundredfold, although whether it is as effective as 'Mummery's Blood'—equal parts of navy rum and Bovril, served piping hot—I cannot say since I have not yet tried the latter. According to W. H. Murray it 'lowers angles, shortens distances and improves weather', so it must be good. Two-thirds of the way round a long walk some years ago I was revived by a cocktail of egg, milk and whisky, but the distance still to be covered remained the same and the assistance proved merely transient. On the other hand, the consumption of glucose at exactly the right moment can often level out quite steep slopes, although it doesn't work so well with overhangs.

It should hardly be necessary to write of the rewards of getting into the hills or what to look for. Obviously, there is so much more to see than from the country lanes but many people go about the hills without using their eyes, except to study the track ahead. I find it interesting to identify all the peaks visible around the horizon from each summit which, even to an experienced Lake District walker, is not always particularly easy—especially from slightly unfamiliar viewpoints. Sometimes, map and compass may have to be consulted. Distant tarns, woods, waterfalls, crags and farms can also be identified and it will often be found that a certain type of lighting will reveal unsuspected features. Interesting approaches to summits or rewarding climbing or scrambling routes can sometimes be found in this way. The amateur geologist or botanist will find almost unlimited scope for exercising his knowledge; I once sat down on the side of St Sunday Crag and discovered about thirty types of flowers and plants within a tiny area, while I have friends who can enthuse about the different kinds of grass, heather and lichen. The sheep, too, are interesting—Herdwicks, with sad, white faces, Swaledales, Roughs and cross-breds—and the walker should try to learn something of the fell farmer's year. To watch the sheep being brought down from the fells for the dipping or the shearing can be one of the delights of a walk in the hills, for the work of the shepherd with three or four dogs combing a fellside, is completely fascinating. The walker, too, should be on the lookout for foxes, red deer, fell ponies, mountain hares and the rest of the wildlife of the district, while, for the bird-watcher, there can be a whole range of wonderment in the hills. The golden eagle now nests in eastern Lakeland but if you happen to be in the area in April or May when they are nesting, or later when they may be feeding their young, please co-operate with the wardens who are trying to ensure that these magnificent birds, which last nested in the area nearly 200 years ago, do not desert their new Lakeland home.

Walkers may find it interesting to study the old walls that criss-cross the fells, some of them hundreds of years old—how they are made and how they stand up to the weather. Sheep-trods, too, may repay a little study—narrower than walkers' tracks and contouring the fellsides without getting anywhere that matters to people, but clearly important to sheep. Old mines and quarries are also interesting places, although inexperienced people should keep away from open shafts and holes where serious accidents, and even fatalities, have occurred. These are just a few of the things to be seen in the hills, little things, very often, that add so much to the enjoyment of the day. It may be no more than an old pony track, levelled by the miners a hundred years ago and now grassed over, a superb bathing pool in a rowan-screened mountain ravine, the remains of an old sheepfold or a useful cave below a familiar crag. But they all add up to one's increasing knowledge of the district and, with the sight of cloud shadows chasing across sunlit fells or of the mist suddenly torn from the ridge ahead, often transform mere exercise into wonderment and even magic.

In later chapters I will try to tell of my feeling for mountains, the beauty and adventure to be enjoyed in the hills, especially on long days, and something of the challenge of strenuous expeditions on the heights and the delights of steep rock. But even for the modest mountain walker, out for the ascent of Coniston Old Man or Skiddaw, the hills offer much more than healthy exercise, and can provide memories to last a lifetime. Mountains, in all weathers and at all seasons, can be a way of life to the faithful. In a changing world, these largest monuments of nature help us to retain a proper sense of proportion and preserve real values that will never fade.

AN EXCITING CORNER

One of the most exciting corners of the fell country is the hummocky area of low, craggy hills and scattered woodlands in the shadow of Wetherlam, just south of the Brathay. Here is a tangled countryside of trees and tarns, of old farmhouses with rickety spinning galleries, long-deserted quarries, tunnels and shafts, and the most tremendous man-made holes in the district. There are vaulted caverns big as cathedrals and underground passages through the fells—hacked out by men hundreds of years ago and now so disguised by nature they are part of the landscape. You can step out of a wood of birch and blackthorn and find yourself on the brink of a man-made cliff, or crawl through some dark tunnel and discover an underground lake that has never seen the sun. From the top of the heather-covered fells you look down on the Wrynose track that the Romans knew and everything about the area—the ancient yews by the whitewashed farmsteads, the little tarns that once provided water power for the quarries, the abandoned spoil heaps grown over with juniper, briar and mountain flowers—speaks of the distant past. This was the country that Lanty Slee, the district's most famous whisky smuggler, knew so well, and here, in caves in the quarries and the woods, he made the fiery stuff he sold more than a century ago for ten shillings a gallon. There were other things to see as well one recent autumn day—a pair of heron languidly taking off from a marshy pool, a buzzard circling the crags, and a fox, on his way from a lonely reconnaisance, sneaking boldly home through the bracken.

3

Steep Rock

Handholds to a Way of Life

The first time I fell off a rock-climb was a year or so before I started proper climbing—I needed the interval in which to recover. The climb is unlisted in the guide-books, a bit of a crag on the slopes of Caw, that lovely little fell on the walk from Woodland to the Coniston tops, and I fell because I was racing my brother up the fellside and, choosing the crag as a short cut, had grabbed for a hold which came away, depositing me, rather painfully, at the foot of the rocks. There was a sprain or two and a bit of blood, but nothing serious, and, before very long, such is the confidence of youth, I was back in the hills again, thirsting for something better. Our first practice ground—still before graduating to 'proper' climbing—was a slab of slaty rock, with a prominent nose on top, on the side of The Hoad near Ulverston, and here we tried to teach ourselves climbing—wearing rubber-soled town shoes, for we couldn't afford proper climbing boots and had not realized that gym-shoes were the more accepted form. We did things on that slab I would not dream of tackling today and one day—unroped, for my 50-foot length of worn Beale was to come later—we managed, in great fear and trembling, to get over the nose.

The tale of my first day's 'real' climbing—on Dow Crag in 1928 with that fine climber and lovable personality, George Basterfield, who was, I think, Mayor of Barrow at the time—is told elsewhere.* This sunny, summer's day, so long ago but still remembered in every detail, affected the rest of my life. Because kindly old George was good enough to take a raw teenager, without any athletic

* *In Mountain Lakeland* (Guardian Press).

ability, up Woodhouse's Route, down Easter Gully, up Arête, Chimney and Crack and down Great Gully just because I had asked him, in the Mayor's Parlour, how to go about getting a pair of boots nailed, I was admitted as a humble novice into the exciting world of climbing. To George, who kept me under his wing for some time, I owe the joy that followed of many hundreds of days on the crags, the discovery of scores of things about rocks and mountains that matter, and the company of a host of interesting people who accepted a rather naïve adolescent because I was a friend of George—and because they were that sort of folk. Through George I was accepted into the company at the Wastwater Hotel, just after the era when the antics in the billiards room had ended but when the same climbers, some of them links with the very earliest days of Lakeland mountaineering, were still around. I used to sit in the drawing-room—the billiards table had recently been removed—or in the little smoke-room, and listen enthralled to the conversation about famous ascents all over the world and join, shyly, in the rollicking singsongs. There were recitations, too, and the telling of tall stories—middle-aged and elderly men of substance and distinction spinning the most unlikely yarns, dressing up, or performing dexterous feats of balance or agility. There were several professors, scholars and literary men—one of them was said regularly to solve the Torquemada crossword puzzle in *The Observer* without reference books—and the talk was often brilliant and far above the head of an ignorant youth. I remember one evening when one of them, presumably to get rid of me, challenged me to run up and down Scafell Pike from the hotel in an hour and, hoping to distinguish myself, I took him on right away. After all these years I can't remember how long I took—much more than an hour, I'm sure—but the memory of the back-breaking ascent—after a big dinner—and the breakneck run down, with sweat in my eyes, is still with me. They gave me a drink when I staggered in, but there was no public acclaim for my stupid performance, and the great men got on with their solemn discussions of more important matters.

On another evening at Wasdale I was introduced by some senior mountaineers into the joys of bathing without a costume or towel, a practice I have adopted on many occasions since. We went to a little pool in the woods near Down-in-the-Dale, stripped off, had a quick dip, and then immediately pulled our dry clothes on to our streaming wet bodies. In this way, I was assured, the water entered the pores with beneficial result and, if the bathe was followed by a brisk trot, the clothes were not dampened and one felt curiously invigorated. They said the method had been invented by a German scientist and was an almost certain cure for many ailments. Probably they were only pulling my leg but, at the time, I believed every word and wondered why towels had ever been invented. Certainly one's clothes slipped on easily enough and they never seemed damp afterwards, but whether this sort of bathing has any advantages, other than those of convenience, I am now inclined to doubt. But I still never bother with costume or towel for tarn bathes, the only snag being that you have to choose your time and place. It is surprising, however, what you can achieve if you are quick and agile. I once had a surreptitious dip, without a costume or towel, in the Lingmell Beck while processions were moving over the high stile a few yards away, and on another occasion I bathed in complete nudity and safety in a pool of the Derwent near Seathwaite Farm less than twenty feet away from returning walkers of both sexes on the Stockley Bridge track. After these slightly dicey adventures it is child's play to bathe, without accoutrements, in places like Hard Tarn underneath Nethermost Pike where hardly anybody goes, although this is the coldest Lakeland bathing I have so far endured.

Only once can I remember being put to any slight embarrassment by the absence of a costume. Several of us had been climbing on Pavey Ark and, on the way down to the valley, stopped for a bathe—costumeless—in Stickle Tarn which, I remember, was cold enough to discourage lengthy immersion. Just when we were about to emerge we spotted a long procession of what, at some distance, appeared to be middle-aged ladies, climbing out of Mill Gill along the track that circles the tarn. Nothing daunted—for the ladies were far enough away to have needed binoculars to see anything even remotely interesting—we started to wade out in the shallow water, when we heard, from the leader of the advancing ladies, the peremptory and stentorian command: 'Get down.' Immediately, such is the power of outraged feminity, we complied, sinking down in the now icy water to observe the decencies, and so remained, shivering, for several minutes until it slowly dawned upon us that the order had been to the procession and not to ourselves. For, indeed, when we studied the ladies in more detail we could see that they had all gone to ground, kneeling or lying down, their backs to the tarn, to save themselves from the terrible sight of half a dozen naked men more than a hundred yards away. This was long before the days of 'total frontal nudity' in stage shows and magazines and before 'Women's Lib' had been invented, but we seized the opportunity to emerge with great relief. We often wondered who these very proper ladies were, and if they happen to read this I hope they will agree that all sides acted with the greatest decorum—although quite unnecessarily so.

But to return to rock-climbing. Dow Crag—and, to a lesser extent, the Langdale crags—was our home ground, and the Wasdale climbs were generally reserved for the holidays. As a result, even today Dow Crag seems a familiar, friendly place whereas the cliffs of Scafell, often visited in our youth on bad days and never thoroughly explored, still have about them an air of mystery and, sometimes, of menace. This might date back to two incidents: the first, an injury to my brother when scrambling on Scafell which involved a rescue party and a stitching-up later by a climbing doctor on the floor of the hall at the Wastwater Hotel; and the second, an accident to George Basterfield on Black Crag above Brown Tongue. George had invited me to join him for a week's climbing at Wasdale but a day or two beforehand I had a letter from him, in curious spidery writing, which stated that he had had a 'bit of an accident', had had to write the letter with his left hand, and was sorry but would not be able to climb with me. He had, however, found a substitute in George Sansom—the man who had partnered Herford on the first ascent of Central Buttress in 1914—who happened to be staying alone at the hotel. I have written elsewhere of the wonderful week I had with Sansom, one of the neatest climbers I have ever seen, and it was some time later when I heard the full story of George's 'bit of an accident'. Apparently he had been climbing on Black Crag with a leader who fell off on a hard move, finishing, without serious injury, some distance below his second. In the process of arresting the fall of his leader, however, George had managed to get a coil of rope twisted round his right thumb and the ensuing conversation has passed into climbing history. 'Are you all right?' shouted up the leader when he had pulled himself together and assessed his bruises. 'No,' said George. 'I've lost me bloody thumb.' And so he had, or at least the top of it, although he told me afterwards that he felt no pain at the time, but merely astonishment.

But although Scafell remained a slightly sinister crag and Dow always a friendly one, it was on the latter that I had my second fall—this time without any damage for I was on the rope. Three of us had made the first ascent, a week earlier, of a rather delicate little route on B Buttress we called Tiger Traverse and were keen on putting up another first ascent of a crack on the left wall of Easy Gully that we had already named, with good reason, Blasphemy Crack. The leader, after a struggle, eventually got up the crack and so did the second, but by the time it came to my turn it had started to rain. I skated about in my rubber plimsolls on the wet rock for some time without making much progress but by now the shower had become a downpour and it was obvious that I wasn't going to get up in rubbers. The only thing to do was to descend and change into nails, but when I had got about halfway up the climb in my 'iron boots' the difficulties proved too much for my technique and I came on to the rope and swung across the face. My companions by now were wet through and I was rapidly losing interest in the route so I was lowered unceremoniously to the foot of the climb and we called it a day. Not only did I fail to climb Blasphemy Crack on its first ascent that September day in 1931 but I have never climbed it since, although I have been told it is an excellent, rather strenuous route. I merely mention the incident now because it was my second fall on a rock-climb —and also my last. There were later occasions when I fell off boulders—the Pudding Stone was one—but this happens to most people, for boulders are things on which you can practise desperate moves without bothering very much about the consequences. The point I am trying to make is that in a lifetime of climbing I have only twice fallen—once through my own negligence on a stupid scramble, and once on to the rope—although there have been several occasions when, as second man, I have found a tight rope more than comforting. This almost complete immunity from accident or injury on the crags—all my mountain injuries have been sustained skiing—may suggest extreme caution, timidity, lack of drive or even superb skill, although this last possibility may be immediately discounted. But it also suggests that climbing cannot really be a dangerous sport. I climbed regularly for more than forty years—for a long time, every weekend—and am still capable of getting up the more amiable routes. At one time, I suppose, I would be doing something like 150 climbs a year but even putting the average over the years as low as 50 this works out at more than 2,000 rock climbs, at up to very severe standard, completed without accident or injury. Most of these climbs, too, were done when protection was nothing like so thorough as it is now, when pegs, nuts, slings, karabiners and hand-jams were either unknown or unused, and when unprotected run-outs of 100 feet of rope were fairly common.

Climbing before the war you just could not, as leader, afford to fall. We used to take a very long time over difficult moves, working them out with great care before committing ourselves, and leaving them to another day if they seemed too hard or we were off form. Nowadays, with protection sometimes arranged every few feet, and greatly advance techniques and equipment, climbing is certainly safer, although very much harder routes are achieved. We would make really desperate moves on boulders a few feet from the ground which we would not dare to repeat on proper rock-climbs, but nowadays these sort of moves are regularly done on the crags in comparative safety, because climbers are able to arrange much better protection, and because climbing standards are very much higher. Climbing is not, therefore, a dangerous sport but is a sport with considerable apparent danger. And it is in the correct assessment of this apparent danger and its reduction to reasonable limits by the exercise of judgement, experience, technique and equipment, that the fascination of the sport lies. Climbers are no braver than golfers or fishermen and, indeed, the best of them may appear to be careful, and even cautious, people. The dash of, for instance, the ski-racer is not needed in climbing and could even be a handicap, for the climber must weigh up every move with the greatest care. Climbers are often frightened or, at least, worried, but the best of them exult in awkward situations for these present them with the opportunity to use their techniques to the utmost, while the supreme joy and well-being which follow the completion of a particularly hard move or climb are rewards that people engaged in less exciting sports can rarely enjoy and understand.

Climbers can sometimes be frightened in very easy places—at least I can—for the main difficulties are often psychological rather than technical. You know the next move is well within your capability but, if you are temporarily 'off form' or emotionally out of tune with the exposure, you hesitate, begin to worry and then start thinking of possible disaster. Sometimes, when you are standing on small holds, your calf muscles begin to judder, and this doesn't help. A great friend of mine, whose name is listed in the guidebooks as the leader of several first ascents, used to be so affected, on his off-days, that he would be quite incapable of climbing just a few feet above the screes on Dow Crag on the easiest of routes. And yet, a day or two later, he would be perfectly at ease on a very severe. I can remember two occasions, on climbs in the lower grades of difficulty, when I felt so scared—for no reason whatever—that I thought I would fall out of sheer fright. On the first, I was leading Abbey Buttress on Great Gable—a fairly steep but perfectly straightforward climb—when I took too long in working out a slightly awkward move, got a leg-judder through standing too long on small holds and, with a fairly long run-out of rope, found I had not the courage either to advance or retreat. I don't know what would have happened to me if a climber on the screes far below had not realized the situation and, quickly, scampered up the fell, got above me and lowered a looped rope. His name was C. J. Astley Cooper, a fine climber and kindly man who died several years ago, and I will always be grateful to him for his prompt and speedy action.

The second occasion was even more inexplicable. I was leading Green Chimney below the Crow's Nest on B Route on Gimmer Crag—a route I must have led a dozen times earlier for in those days we were always running up and down the Gimmer 'Alphabet'—when suddenly, in a very easy place, I felt rooted to the rock and quite unable to go up or down. It was a curious and terrible feeling for, although the only way you could fall from this place would be by just letting go and dropping down, I suddenly felt as if I was scrabbling about on the side of a church steeple without a ladder. The situation was explained to my patient second who advised me to stand quite still for a while, close my eyes, and then, after a rest, 'get up the bloody thing', which I eventually did but I have never been so frightened on climbs several times harder. A few days later, on very much harder climbs, I felt heartily ashamed of my performance which I can only put down either to a hangover, indigestion or an over-active imagination. Indeed, lack of imagination can be a great asset in difficult climbing; it doesn't help to be too much aware of your situation or the consequences if you happened to let go—and certainly not in the days when we climbed without slings and nuts and bits of wire. I remember, in 1948, watching Jim Birkett lead the first ascent of Haste Not, a very severe and exposed route up the overhangs in White Gill, Langdale. He was on the sensational third pitch and, after some delicate moves, reached up for a hold to pull himself up and, as he was doing so, hesitated for a moment, in a completely off-balance position, and seemed about to fall. Down in the gully we held our breath—it seemed a desperate situation—and then, in a moment, he was up. We were immensely relieved for disaster had seemed imminent, but all that happened was that Jim shouted down: 'Did you see that? I reached up for a bloody hold, but there wasn't one there at all. Thought I was off. Never laughed so much for years.' He thought it very funny; we, standing in safety, had had our hearts in our mouths. They say it's all in the mind.

On some days—but not many, in my case—even hard climbs seem easy. The holds are there, even if minuscule, and all you have to do is to use them and get up. Sometimes, on rare occasions, in perfect weather and on good form, we have wandered about the crags, eschewing recognized routes and delicately exploring to right and left, tasting the supreme joy of complete confidence and fitness on steep rock. But one also remembers other days when things seemed desperate and you secretly swore that, if you emerged unscathed, you would give up climbing for good. The climb that at the time seemed the hardest thing I had ever done was Hangover on Dove Crag, a steep route of character, very exposed at the top. I have done several routes, both before this climb and later, that are supposed to be more difficult than Hangover, but I found the third pitch steep, strenuous and delicate, all at the same moment, and felt very grateful that I was not leading. Although I have led harder moves I could not have led this one—certainly not that day, anyway. For me the climb was well-named for I was suffering at the time from the after-effects of a celebration, at the Old Dungeon Ghyll Hotel, of an attempt by some friends on the Lakeland 24 hours fell record. The attempt had failed, through bad weather, but nobody was depressed about it and the merriment went on happily for many hours. The next morning Hangover was selected as an appropriate route but I announced that I was in no condition to climb, although agreed to be persuaded to accompany the others to the foot of the crag where they promised I would be left in peace. It seemed important at least to see the route for I was supposed to be collaborating in the production of a guide-book to the area and the others agreed to describe and measure the pitches for me. Guide-book authors and their assistants may climb all the routes themselves nowadays but at that time my fellow-collaborator and I had decided that, since the hardest climbs were beyond us, it would be perfectly proper, and indeed essential, to employ more competent climbers to do these for us. This arrangement worked very well for a time, but when we realized that people were putting up new routes of increasing severity nearly every weekend and that the chances of our ever repeating them seemed remote, we asked to be relieved of our commitment. To hire more able friends to do a few routes might have been all right, but to be forced to leave the assessment of most of the climbs to others seemed to be pushing absentee guide-book writing too far. So we chickened out.

But I was still involved on the Hangover day and pictured myself lazing away the afternoon at the foot of the climb, while I slowly recovered from my thick head. The walk to the crag proved rather trying and the ascent of the screes to the foot of the crag about as much as I could manage, but worse was to come for my heartless companions poured scorn on my indisposition and, after much bullying and many threats, forced me to tie on and climb the thing. One little thing that didn't help was the discovery, lying on the ground at the foot of the climb, of a rusty, home-made piton of unusual length that I thought had probably been used in desperation on some particularly awkward move and had then fallen out. The hour that followed is sharply etched in my memory but does not need recalling. The others did not seem to find the climb particularly demanding, but I had to be cajoled and dragged up it in a more or less comatose state, swearing that I'd never climb with any of them again. But of course I did and, really, I'm very grateful to them for taking me up what, I'm sure, for a competent and sober climber, is a very fine route.

Dow Crag, as I have written, was our happy hunting ground and for several years we were up there nearly every weekend. We lived in a wooden hut—a converted garage—in a field near the lake shore at Coniston Old Hall farm, sleeping on rough wooden bunks we had made ourselves and cooking on ancient primus stoves. In those days in the late 1920s and early 1930s we did not possess sleeping bags but used blankets we had 'borrowed' from our homes. These were stored in a tin trunk in the hut and seemed nearly always damp, while for mattresses we mostly used coils of old climbing ropes or any bits of padding we could find. It may be that the rheumatic and assorted muscular pains that have assailed some of us in later years could be attributed to these early rather damp and uncomfortable nights, although at the time we thought nothing of it, glorying in our fitness. We called our little club, with misplaced over-confidence, the Coniston Tigers, but only one of us was anything like a 'tiger' and, after a very bad fall, he never climbed again. Gradually we worked our way through the little red guide-book until we had done almost every route on the crag, including the Eliminates, although our lone 'tiger' was the only one to do Black Wall. Once we were nearly benighted on the crag but finally got down to our torches in the cave by a perilous, roped descent of Easy Terrace in the pitch darkness—perhaps the only time that this easy scramble has ever been done on a rope.

On another occasion we climbed down Woodhouse's Route roped to a cragfast sheep, but we thought little of this, for we had done Woodhouse's under every conceivable condition including darkness, snow and ice. This is the climb that I have done more often than any other—mostly because on really bad days when everything else seemed impossible we used to do this as a sort of gesture. We had a trick of finishing one of the pitches feet first, although we also fell off it more than once without hurting ourselves. The climb was only regarded as a 'difficult' in those days and it was with some surprise, and not a little satisfaction, that I saw that in the latest guide-books it has been upgraded to 'hard very difficult'—one of the few examples of old classics getting harder over the years, or at least being judged harder. Other examples are Eagle's Nest Direct and Kern Knotts Crack on Great Gable which have been upgraded from severe to mild very severe, and deservedly so in my opinion. We once did Kern Knotts Crack and the nearby Innominate Crack one after the other and I certainly found Kern Knotts Crack the harder of the two, although the Innominate has always been regarded as a worthy very severe.

Looking back on these early days I remember we lived for rock-climbing, counting the days before the weekends. We had little patience then for fell-walking on its own as a day out, except when the weather was very bad, but, in fairness to us, we normally finished a climbing day on Dow, and on many of the other crags, with a walk home over the tops. And I have a hundred memories of trotting down the fells in the evening sunlight, with the shadows lengthening across the turf and the larks singing and the sun setting over the sea, which will always be with me. We climbed in cheap, black, worn plimsolls—deliberately purchased, for about one and sixpence, a size too small—when the rocks were dry, and in clinker-nailed boots when they were wet. Climbing-wear was cord breeches and old tweed jackets and we had no waterproof clothing, except capes and sou'westers for the fells. I remember once meeting Graham Macphee on Gable Crag when he showed me an 'anorak' he had invented which consisted of an old mackintosh with an arrangement of cords by which he could convert a raincoat into a climbing jacket. The manilla ropes we used became very stiff, heavy and unmanageable when wet and the introduction of nylon ropes, perhaps twenty years later, came as a boon and a blessing. We had no slings or karabiners and either tied ourselves on to the rock or used thread belays. The unprotected run-outs were, of course, the length of the pitch.

It is difficult, out of hundreds of wonderful days, to remember the best, but we once did all the Napes ridges in one day and would frequently do at least half a dozen climbs on Dow in one visit. The first day I led Eagle's Nest on Great Gable, with George Basterfield as second, was a memorable occasion for the Abraham photograph of A. E. Field on the arête, which used to hang in the Wastwater Hotel, had always impressed and rather frightened me. But with George behind, to explain every move and to give confidence, it went easily enough. The days with George Sansom, who used barley sugar to make his fingers stick on the smaller holds, were also exciting and revealing and with him I did my first very severe—North West on Pillar. Sansom was one of the neatest and quickest climbers I have ever seen but he went up fellsides more slowly than anybody else—to conserve his strength. His excruciatingly slow ascent of Gavel Neese, for example, used to be achieved almost without visible motion. On the other hand his descent of Napes Needle used to be a miracle of controlled speed.

But most days were with friends with whom we climbed every weekend, and we were well accustomed to one another's idiosyncrasies. Some of us enjoyed slimy chimneys, others were at their best in cracks or pulling over overhangs; I was happiest on slabs with small holds, and climbs like South West on Pillar, when in good form, were a joy. It would be impossible to select one's favourite climb but I think I would say that in my humble opinion New West on Pillar is the best of the easier climbs in the Lake District. It is long, steep, varied and the easiest way up a very fine face—a natural, as distinct from an artificial, route. I remember being slightly disconcerted on the climb on one occasion when I

Skiddaw from High Rigg

Wetherlam from Langdale Pikes

Bannerdale Crags from Souther Fell

reached the little chimney at the top to find a bottle, labelled 'Human Plasma', hanging at the back of the cleft. Other curious objects discovered on climbs have included a pair of lady's knickers hanging from a final pitch on Shepherd's Crag, a metal notice reading 'Public Footpath' bolted on to Middefell Buttress—perhaps a fairly accurate description—and a pair of climbing boots on the footholds below the 'Brant and Slape' move on Pavey Ark—just as if their owner had been plucked out of them and translated into the upper air.

Other excellent routes in the lower grades might include Bowfell Buttress, Little Chamonix on Shepherd's Crag, Moss Gill on Scafell, Gimmer Chimney, and Tophet Bastion on the Napes, while in the middle grades some favourites would be Central Chimney, Intermediate Gully and Murray's Route on Dow, C, D and E on Gimmer, Jones' Route on Scafell Pinnacle, Tophet Wall and, perhaps Fortiter on Grey Crag in Birkness Combe. I have never done a climb in the extremely severe class, and will never do one now, but among the ordinary very severes I have particularly enjoyed have been the Eliminates on Dow, White Gill Wall, North West on Pillar and dear old Eagle's Nest. Smuggler's Chimney on Great Gable has now, I noticed, been advanced about three grades to very severe—a very reassuring state of affairs. When I did it about forty years ago it was only supposed to be an ordinary severe and not the sort of climb on which to waste much time. It seemed to me at the time, however, about the most strenuous thing I had ever done—mostly because I had a guide-book in my breast pocket which made my width exactly the same as the chimney. How well-endowed young women get up this thing remains one of life's little mysteries.

More people come to grief on the fells in the Lake District than on the crags but there are still many beginners whose approach to rock-climbing is far too casual. We are all familiar with the growing number of walkers lost in the mist without map or compass, or the ability how to use them, and people in gum-boots or low shoes falling off Helvellyn, but there are also cases of completely inexperienced youngsters tackling severe or very severe rock climbs—because they've seen somebody else doing them. One admires their spirit while deploring their lack of common sense. Rock-climbing is a highly technical sport, with many rules, most of which cannot easily be put down on paper but must be learned by experience. Sometimes, on perfectly dry rock, they might manage to get up their chosen climb, by good luck rather than good management, but the next time, on slightly damp rock, or an awkward move they haven't met before or even knocked off balance by a gust of wind, they either come to grief or get cragfast. I still believe the old-fashioned nailed boots we used to wear provided us with the best possible apprenticeship on steep rock. You learned by long experience the exact safety angle of the foot and leg to the rock, how to step up out of balance, and how to keep the body away from the crag, but with modern footgear beginners are liable just to place their feet on the rock and hope for the best, which may be all right in perfect conditions but can be highly dangerous at other times. It seems to me to be more important to learn the rules in rock-climbing than in golf, tennis or football, for mistakes can have more serious results, but the only way to learn them is by constant practice on easy routes or in the company of an experienced leader. Handbooks on technique may be helpful for improving your style, but you can only learn it properly on rock and the knowledge should be acquired gradually. Apropos of technique it has always surprised me that so much emphasis is sometimes placed, in the earliest stages of instruction, on methods of abseiling, which seems rather like putting the cart before the horse. I have even heard of walkers being given instruction in the controlled descent of steep crags on the rope which savours to me of a gimmick, rather than a necessary accomplishment. Climbers should certainly know how to abseil, but many other things should be learned first, and it is far better that teachers planning to take children walking in the hills should teach them how to use map and compass really well rather than give them instruction in roped descents from crags.

Looking back over a lifetime of rock-climbing—much of it of a fairly modest nature—I am satisfied that it has had an enormous affect on my enjoyment of the hills. Valley views are much more dramatic and exciting when seen from halfway up a crag, and climbing takes you into corners that the fell walker never sees. Tens of thousands of words have been written to try to explain why men climb steep rocks or high mountains and I do not feel it necessary to add greatly to the total. Most of us climb simply because we enjoy it, and there seems no need to analyse our reasons. I have nearly always lived in sight of the hills and feel strangely depressed and unfulfilled in flat country. If asked to explain, in as few words as possible, the attraction of mountains I would probably say: 'Beauty and adventure.' Like many other climbers I started by first exploring the hills—mostly, no doubt, in a search for beauty, but also in the hope of adventure. Waterfalls, old mine workings, disused quarries and caves and minor rock outcrops were obvious attractions and when most of the Lake District mountains had been ascended by walking it seemed natural to graduate to the crags. For the amount of adventure to be won from a walk over the familiar fells—except in winter or in bad weather—can become rather limited and a spirited youngster may feel the need for something more demanding. He still appreciates the beauty—if he has started by seeking it out—but he now wants the adventure as well. And so he takes up rock climbing. Very soon he will discover that he is involved in a very precise kind of sport. Just as in golf, he will find that it is sometimes fractions of an inch that matter, the exact placing of a boot, the particular shaping of the hands or fingers, the studied balance of the body. But a mistake or a misjudgement in climbing can be more serious than in golf and so the climber achieves a very high level of concentration. You can be sloppy and lackadaisical when playing golf or walking the hills but you can't climb rocks this way—at least, not when you are leading.

I think it is also true to say that you cannot climb rocks if you are worried or thinking about something else—certainly not to a high standard. To lead successfully a difficult pitch—or even to follow—means that you have devoted the whole of your skill, intelligence, imagination and technique to the problem, to the exclusion of everything else. Nothing in the world matters except the negotiation of the next few feet—perhaps, indeed, the successful use of one key hold. And since the mental and physical output is often so high it follows that the satisfaction, the release from tension, that follows the successful completion of the pitch, climb or mountain is tremendous. Golfers may win immense satisfaction from sinking a ten-feet putt; how much greater is the inner reward for successfully surmounting the final ten feet of a difficult pitch, poised perhaps hundreds of feet above the screes. And this is all it is—the inner reward. There are no spectators—unless the climber is taking part in a 'TV Spectacular', which most of us think distasteful—and, apart from a grunt of satisfaction or relief from his second, the whole reward is the wonderful feeling of well-being and confidence that quietly envelops you. You have got up and nothing else matters—except the next pitch.

This is the real reward but there are so many by-products—the successful deployment of techniques, the delicate precision of careful foot and finger work, the exhilarating downward views, the smoke in the heather or on a couch of bilberries at the top, the tremendous feeling of physical fitness, and the great joy of dangers shared. This last, comradeship, is one of the greatest gifts in climbing. To climb with a companion, roped together, on difficult rock implies considerable mutual trust and respect, and generally warm friendship. Climbing friends are often friends of a lifetime. You have shared risks and discomfort and you each know the best and worst of the other. At times you trust your life with your companion, and you have to know that he will not let you down. Climbers can have first-class rows afterwards in hut or tent, but rarely squabble on a climb; other things are much more important. To most of us who go into the hills and on to the crags our climbing friends are always slightly special, in a different category from friends from other walks of life. To meet them brings back memories of the mountains that to the real climber mean more to him than almost anything else.

Rock-climbing, or course, is only a small part of mountaineering, although to some it is a sport on its own. I have written earlier that the climber, after he has become too old and decrepit for the harder climbs, generally goes back to the hills to walk the heights rather than scale the cliffs. But his rock-climbing training stands him in good stead for he has won the real freedom of the fells. Not for him the popular walks along well-trodden paths for he must be seeking out new ways, looking round corners and discovering out-of-the-way places. As a climber he knows exactly where he can go and what he can do. He is not deterred by a crag or gully, either above or below him, but will know how to tackle it safely or avoid it with circumspection. Remote, untrodden Scottish bens, guarded by crags or snow, are within his province for he knows his capabilities and his limitations, can use map, compass, ice-axe and crampons and, if he is an all-round mountaineer, his skis. He may no longer be able to climb the more difficult rock routes but he can size up a mountain or a cliff and know what to do about it. His knowledge of pitons, nuts and etriers may be rusty or lacking altogether but he knows whether or not he can get up or down a fifty-foot crag or whether a nasty-looking gully is impracticable or not. His clothes may look a bit ancient, his ice-axe old-fashioned, and his boots rather clumsy but he is still a free man of the hills, well able to go in safety where he chooses, and still seeking, and finding, beauty and adventure.

MOSES' TROD

The easiest way up Great Gable for the infirm or lazy is from a parked car on top of Honister Pass—a gently undulating walk of about three miles, with less than two thousand feet of ascent and the reward of changing views every few hundred yards. The other day I passed an old gentleman of perhaps 80 pottering along quite comfortably in the sunshine and I've no doubt four-year-olds—with the inducement of some small reward—could do it. It is, though, rather a dry walk on a warm day, with few sizeable becks and no opportunity for a quick bathe—unless you seek out the pools on Grey Knotts—so that the distant views of lakes and tarns are particularly tantalizing. A week ago there was a nice patch of old snow in a ravine on the side of Green Gable to provide a cool interlude but elsewhere, in one of the sunniest May weeks for years, it could have been a sultry day in high summer. The fells shimmered in the heat haze, insects whirred in the dry grass, dust rose from the scree runs, and the rocks were warm to the touch. On the top, people were dozing in the sunshine or looking with wonder across the trough of Wasdale to the snow on the Scafells. Windy Gap—a Piccadilly Circus of routes—had been populous but Beck Head was deserted and the dark carpet of conifers in Ennerdale seemed spread over an empty valley. I took the old track across the fells that the whisky smugglers, the wad thieves, or the honest quarrymen once used, and sat in a corner of rock high above Moses' Trod watching two climbers tackling the steep exposure of Engineers' Slabs on the shadowed face of Gable Crag. Their confident voices came winging down into the combe, making me feel ashamed of my laziness.

4

The Magic of Skye

Adventures in a Mountain Paradise

We first went to Skye in the early 1930s—two of us in an open Morris Minor that had cost me £40. Somewhere between Broadford and Sligachan it sprung a leak but I mended the hose with electrician's tape and this was the only trouble we had in a thousand miles of motoring. This was a journey to a magical island that I had been reading about for years and it completely fulfilled every expectation. I can remember now, although it was forty years ago, the sunlit morning drive along the side of Loch Lomond, the speedy exhilaration of the new highway through Glencoe, the sight of red deer from the old road over to Glen Shiel, the Five Sisters of Kintail and lovely Loch Duich, the steep descent to the old Dornie ferry—now replaced by a bridge—and my first sight of the Cuillin hills from the winding road to the Kyle of Lochalsh. Much of the old road to the isles has now disappeared, replaced by smooth modern highways or drowned by hydro-electro schemes, and some of the old magic has gone. The road, little more than a rough cart-track, that used to wind over tree roots through the Glen Garry woods and the hill road from Tomdoun, with little passing places scratched out of the heather, was a delight. I remember buying a pipe for a shilling in a little store at Shiel Bridge and taking a photograph of the girl who was to become my wife, standing beside an old thatched bothy that has long since disappeared. In a lonely part of Glen Shiel we had a meal of baps and bannocks in the tiny croft of an elderly couple to whom we had an introduction from a distant relative. The old people, who had little English and spoke Gaelic to each other, could not have been kinder if we had been their children, and refused to take anything for their hospitality. But the little, lonely croft was pulled down, or fell down, at least thirty years ago and the Gaelic tongue is disappearing from the glens.

The ferries were primitive and adventurous. We went by Ballachulish because the road by Kinlochleven was either too rough or had not been built—I can't remember which—and you had to have good brakes to stop in time for the old Dornie ferry which was reached by driving up two planks. The Kyle of Lochalsh ferry was equally rickety, and quite tricky to get on and off in wild weather. It cost six shillings in those days which I remember thinking quite exorbitant. But once across the narrow stretch of water, with the gulls swooping and squawking overhead and the smell of the tangle in your nostrils, you were in a new country—a Gaelic-speaking island, with rough roads creeping round a sharply indented coastline, a few scattered, peat-burning crofts, the smoothly rounded Red Hills that guard the sanctuary and, in the south-west corner, the most dramatic mountains in Britain, the Black Cuillin.

There were no bed and breakfast signs in those days, no organized camp sites, no hostels or huts and few stretches of decent road. You drove from Carbost to Glen Brittle with one wheel in a rut and the other in the heather and you stayed at the Lodge, at the Post Office or at Mary Campbell's where all the great men, who had 'discovered' the mountains of Skye only two generations earlier, had stayed. Indeed, it was less than forty years before my first visit that the last of Britain's unclimbed mountains—Sgurr Coire an Lochain, a modest peak near the main Cuillin ridge—had been ascended.

The feeling of being in a different sort of country—although only separated from the mainland by about half a mile of water—was very strong that day in the 1930s when I made the first of very many visits to Skye. There was an old woman scratching the ground outside a blackened cottage that was little more than a hut, but when we asked whether we were on the right road for Glen Brittle she didn't seem to understand us. The road was unsurfaced and full of pot-holes, necessitating very slow progress, but was almost a race-track compared with the bumpy crawl over the hillside to Glen Brittle which once threw a friend of mine out of a sidecar into the heather. And the road to the Cuillin was not only unsurfaced and bumpy but also incredibly circuitous, for, in order to make a mile or two of progress towards a sighted objective, you had to drive ten miles or so round the sea lochs that seemed to bite deeply into the island every time you turned a corner. At first we were disappointed with the hills we saw—rounded, heather-covered and devoid of crags—but, somewhere near the Sligachan Inn, we had our first sight of Sgurr nan Gillean and the northern end of the Cuillin ridge and knew we had come to the right place. For these were the most dramatic mountains we had ever seen—a jagged array of spires and pinnacles quite different from the Scottish mainland hills or the fells of our native Lakeland. And when we topped the last rise of the dreadfully rough track from Carbost and began the descent to Glen Brittle we suddenly saw the long line of the Cuillin from Bruach na Frithe to Sgurr Dearg lighted by the setting sun, with blue-shadowed corries and foaming burns leaping down the rocky hillsides. These were the mountains we had come so far to see and we were satisfied. And later that night, after supper, we stepped outside the Lodge to sniff the air and in the darkness, with the ridge showing black against the purple sky, we sensed a stillness and peace, as the mountains went to sleep, that I have rarely experienced since.

The next day, warm and sunny with a fresh breeze coming off the bay, we went up Sgurr Dearg and, from the summit, saw the Outer Hebrides, the nearer islands of Rhum and Canna and half the mountains of northern Scotland. This was the first time we had scrambled on mountains that were rocky nearly all the way up and this seemed to add a new dimension to mountain walking. By then I had been rock-climbing for several years but this was something new—to spend a day going up and down mountains and to be able to keep on rock nearly all the time. I think we only saw one other person all day and that was near the end—a man who asked us where we had been. It was only then that I learned that Dearg is pronounced 'Jerrack', or something like it—my first lesson in Gaelic. I had many lessons later from Mr MacRae at the Lodge and, years afterwards, used to go into his cottage in the evenings for further lessons and for the latest news of the glen. Gaelic is a most difficult language for an Englishman to understand, and, after many years, I have never achieved more than a few simple words, but it is fairly easy to learn how to pronounce the mountain names more or less correctly—a useful accomplishment when you are trying to do the 'Munros'. There are half-a-dozen simple rules, which you can pick up in guide-books, and you can understand fairly quickly why, for instance, Mhadaidh is pronounced 'Vatee' and Ghreadaidh, 'Greeta'. Many of the formidable assortment of consonants in Gaelic are not pronounced; they just seem to be put in to baffle the Sassenach.

Our second day on Skye was to be slightly more ambitious. We had planned to go round the coast by boat to Loch Scavaig, walk along the shore of Loch Coruisk into the very heart of the Cuillin and then climb back over the ridge to Glen Brittle. The one-inch Ordnance Survey map of the Cuillin was not very good forty years ago—it is better now—for it showed so much rock and so many contours that it was almost impossible to see the lie of the mountains, which were obscured anyway by their names. However, I knew there was a pass over the ridge from Coruisk to Glen Brittle—the Bealach Coire na Banachdich, between Sgurr Dearg and Sgurr na Banachdich—and I thought we should be able to find it fairly easily. Hanging on the wall in the hall of Glen Brittle Lodge at that time was a small, fairly rough relief-map of the southern Cuillin and, studying this the previous evening, I had seen that the second tributary of the burn that flows into Loch Coruisk led upwards towards this pass. All we had to do, therefore, I thought naïvely, was to follow this stream to its source and then continue in the same direction and we would find the pass—no matter what the weather. What I had not realized was that scores of streams flow into the Coruisk burn in wet weather, that the relief-map was not a particularly accurate representation, and that the Cuillin, in mist, are much trickier mountains than the familiar Lakeland fells. About ten years before our first visit to Skye a map of the Cuillin, at the convenient scale of three inches to the mile, had been reproduced specially for the Scottish Mountaineering Club from a photographic triangulation by Howard Priestman, but I knew nothing about this map. If I had had a copy I think I could have found the way, even in bad weather and with my almost complete lack of knowledge of the area. Looking now at this map I note it does not show any of the passes across the ridge, as such, but from the contours it can be seen that the route to the 'bealach' we had selected would start about one mile after reaching the head of the loch and just before the entry of the fourth main tributary into the main Coruisk burn.

It was drizzling when we set off and the clouds were down to about 1,000 feet but I didn't think this should deter us. After all, I thought, I had been climbing for years and knew my way about mountains, and we were only going to cross a ridge by a known pass. It should be explained at this point that a pass in the Cuillin bears little resemblance to a Lakeland pass—at least it didn't forty years ago. There were only two or three feasible routes across the ridge and none of them was a track, as we know the term. The passes are on rock and there were no nail scratches although when I was last over the Banachdich 'pass' several years ago the way was marked, here and there, by an occasional cairn consisting—in the Highland fashion—of just two or three small stones perched on boulders or outcrops. To find these cairns in mist, twenty years ago, if you did not know the way, was not always easy and it was probably much more difficult in the 1930s. But at that time I knew nothing about Skye 'passes', only having been up one mountain in the island, and could not imagine any difficulty.

We walked down to Loch Brittle in the rain and met on the shore, by arrangement, a man in oilskins with a tiny boat fitted with an outboard engine. Anoraks, cagoules and other wet-weather equipment were either not in general use in those days or had not been invented, and we were just dressed in old clothes. Whether or not we had capes I can't remember, but I think it unlikely, for by the time we reached the comparative shelter of Loch Scavaig we were pretty wet after a very uncomfortable journey in a choppy sea. We were deposited on the beach at the foot of great streaming slabs that reached up in the mist towards the unseen summit of Gars-bheinn and left, unceremoniously, to our fate. For years we had been reading of the glories and the grandeur of Loch Coruisk, the wildest place, it was said, in Britain, but there was no beauty in the loch or the corrie that morning—just wild waves on a half-seen stretch of water, a wet, mist-filled glen, burns in spate everywhere and black screes and crags rearing up on all sides into the dark, menacing clouds.

But we were young, healthy and optimistic so we trudged for more than a mile along the shore of the loch, through boulders and across the burns and then began to look out for the second tributary running into the main feeder for the loch which I was confident would lead us to the pass over the ridge, 3,000 feet above. It was only after we had passed the head of the loch that we realized the expedition was not going to be the simple affair I had imagined for, instead of three or four burns flowing down the hillside, as shown on the relief map in the Lodge, the whole of the corrie seemed to be alive with the sound of falling waters and there were white torrents racing down through the mist on all sides. Which one of all these wild streams in spate was our ladder to the ridge? I got out my one-inch Ordnance Survey map but it was useless; and I tried to remember the relief map at the Lodge, but without inspiration. We would just have to try to select the most likely-looking burn and follow it; if that proved the wrong one we would try the next.

Having made our choice we trudged up the screes towards the grey blanket of mist, now perhaps 500 feet above our heads, and I told my companion, to encourage her, that we should be on the ridge in an hour or so. But two hours later—it might even have been three hours—we were still not out of the corrie, visibility had been reduced to a few yards, and we had no idea where we were. After following our first chosen tributary, up steep, sliding screes and rock outcrops, to a height approaching 2,000 feet, we had suddenly come to a tremendous rock crevasse barring our way. I have never identified this place since—largely because I have not often climbed on this side of the ridge—but my memory of it, forty years later, is that it was pretty deep, not easily climbable, in and out, and perhaps seven feet wide. With an adventurous male companion I think we would have risked a jump or tried to climb into and out of it, but my companion took one look at it and announced she was going no further—not in that direction, anyway. Obviously, she said, we were on the wrong route, and I had to admit it certainly did not look like a much-traversed pass over the ridge.

So down we went, the way we had come with so much effort, and, back in the corrie, I re-examined the maze of streaming burns, and tried to decide which ones had been newly formed by the recent rain, and, from the remainder, which one might be the key to the pass. And having made my decision, we set off once again, from somewhere near sea-level, to reach the ridge and make our way down the other side to baths, a hot meal, and a cheery fire. Again, it was a steep, slippery trudge through the mist and rain and soon we were in thick cloud and unable to see more than a few yards ahead. We pressed on, seeing no track, cairns or signs of previous passage—the Cuillin was still a fairly remote area forty years ago—and then, suddenly, we hit the ridge. I remember how unexpected it was—

one moment, trudging upwards through the scree, the next, finding ourselves in a narrow gap with a steep drop on the other side. It was exactly how I had pictured the pass—a gap, perhaps six feet wide or less, almost as narrow as a tight-rope, with steep crags soaring up into the mist at either end. We could only see a few feet up the cloud-wreathed crags and a similar distance down the pass on either side, and it seemed a very wild and lonely place indeed. However, we had reached the ridge at last and all that remained to be done was to scramble down the other side into Coire na Banachdich which would lead us straight to the Lodge.

But it was the wrong pass, and probably not a pass at all. We did not realize this until much later when we were climbing down near-vertical chimneys in approaching darkness and had come to the conclusion that even passes in Skye couldn't be like this. We had set off down from the gap in high spirits, hoping to be out of the cloud in half an hour of so, but very soon found ourselves on steep, downward-sloping slabs, cleft at intervals by chimneys and gullies. There seemed no easy way to circumvent the first of the chimneys we encountered so we climbed down it—or rather I climbed down it, after lowering my companion on the rope. Looking back on the whole sorry escapade I am convinced that the only sensible thing I did that day was to take a rope, a precaution I had taken knowing that these were rock mountains, and rather different from our Lakeland fells. I think this is the only time I have ever taken a rope on a mountain walk in summer, without rock-climbing in mind, but I don't know what we would have done without it. My companion was no rock-climber, and in the mist and rain the slabs and chimneys looked quite nasty. By now, of course, we had realized we were certainly not on the route we had planned, that we had no idea where we were, and that it would be dark fairly soon. Speed, it seemed to me, was essential for if we could only get below the mist before nightfall we ought to be able to make a reasonable guess about our position, and eventually retrieve our lost fortunes. So that as soon as my companion began to make heavy weather of the chimneys, losing valuable time, I tied her on the rope and lowered her, as quickly as possible, down each of the difficulties, scrambling down after her in turn. I don't know how many rope lengths we needed—it seemed about twenty but could have been fewer—but I know that long before we had got down the slabs my arms and shoulders were aching with the strain, and I was feeling very tired. By now it was almost dark, but at least we were on easier ground and had got below the clouds.

The story of the remainder of the uncomfortable day, during which we broke most of the rules of mountaineering, is soon told. We scrambled, slipped and squelched in the darkness down the hillside, fell into burns, tore our already tattered clothes, grazed hands and knees and, more than once, tripped headlong in the heather but, at long last, we hit a track that seemed to be going in the right direction. Following this we eventually reached the road through the glen which we followed for about three miles to the Lodge. Mrs MacRae, a kindly old soul, greeted our arrival with expressions of relief for she had been about to alert some sort of a rescue team which in those days probably meant ringing up the police in Portree and hoping for the best. Where they would have searched, with the whole of the Cuillin to go at, I have no idea, for in line with our catalogue of mistakes, we had neglected to give the Lodge details of our intended journey. No doubt the boatman would have recalled that he had last seen us, looking wet and miserable, on the windswept beach of Loch Scavaig, and they would have had to work it out from there. Exactly where we crossed the ridge I have never been able to discover. I think it most likely that we crossed between two of the several peaks of Sgurr a'Mhadaidh and dropped down the crags into Tairneilear and thence into Coire na Creiche, but I've been unable to identify our route or work out how we reached the ridge from Coire an Uaigneis on the Coruisk side. Many mountaineering lessons which I ought to have learned long before were hammered home that day and I hope I have treated the Cuillin with proper respect since.

Following that first visit to Skye in the early 1930s—we spent the remainder of the week soberly exploring the more accessible peaks—I have been back to the island on perhaps a dozen occasions. For a long time we went there every year, often with our children, nearly always staying at the Lodge where we were able to watch a succession of MacRaes running the farm. Memories of so many visits seem to merge into one another but the Lodge has always seemed the same—the cosy fires, the walk across the garden through the gate to the hillside, evening talks in the little parlour with the MacRaes about the latest news in the glen, the boot-cleaning at the back door in the mornings, and the last view of the sleeping hills at night. Some memories, though, are very clear. One year George Spenceley and I were there for a week's climbing and before leaving for the hill one morning George had occasion to go to the toilet. Several minutes later there was a tremendous crash followed by a groan and as I was getting up to see what had happened George walked into the drawing-room with his head streaming with blood. He had been quietly seated, performing his usual matutinal functions and contemplating nothing in particular, as one does on these occasions, when the heavy skylight suddenly crashed down on to his head, for no reason at all. Why it had chosen to fall at just this moment we never found out, but George had to receive medical attention before we could leave for the hill.

Another remembered occasion was also rather bloody. We had our dog Sambo, a friendly Border collie, with us that year and one day he managed to get himself involved in a fight with all the Border collies on the farm—so far as I can remember, about ten of them. There was an appalling din and I rushed out to see Sambo, a most inoffensive animal, being savagely mauled by all the others and Mr MacRae, in the middle of it, belabouring his animals with a stick to try and break up the fight. It was a most unpleasant sight and the result was that poor Sambo was very badly damaged indeed, one of his wounds being a deep tear in his stomach about ten inches long. Why the other dogs had taken such a dislike to him we never found out, although it might have had something to do with the fact that Sambo and the leader of the pack were as alike as two peas in a pod. Anyway, we took Sambo, bleeding profusely, to the vet at Portree, a long drive distant, and various medicaments and stitches were applied, but for some reason the vet refused to stitch up the terrible gaping wound in his stomach. When we got back to Glen Brittle Sambo went to sleep on some rugs and the following day we thought we would try him out on a short walk of a hundred yards or so up the hill. The vet had said that a bit of exercise would not do him any harm. He went very slowly, picking his way carefully, but then seemed to take on a new lease of life and trotted ahead of us. Very soon we had difficulty in keeping up with him, and, to cut a long story short, he eventually led us up the very rocky Coire na Banachdich and eventually on to the summit of Sgurr Dearg—a fairly strenuous walk, there and back, of four or five miles, with more than 3,000 feet of ascent and descent. In a long and adventurous life, Sambo reached the top of many of the Cuillin peaks and almost all the mountains of Lakeland. Apart from having been almost mauled to death by his Glen Brittle pals, he had been swept over waterfalls, fallen 500 feet down a snow slope and been hauled up several rock climbs on a rope. But he finally died in my arms of old age—peacefully, I hope, for he was one of the best of my mountain friends.

With the children we did all the usual expeditions in Skye—driving round the coast to remote rocky beaches, scrambling about on the Quirang and the Storr rocks, walking up to the ridge on blazingly hot days and then bathing luxuriously in Loch Lagan, mingling with the tourists at Dunvegan Castle and making perilous routes up the sea cliffs around the bay. Once we met Dame Flora McLeod when she came to tea at the Lodge and another time we went out in a boat on the bay with Gavin Maxwell who later was to write the highly successful *Ring of Bright Water*. I can't remember how we came to be in his boat—I think he was trying to establish a shark fishery on the island of Soay at the time—but I know he convinced my wife that we had sighted killer whales far out in the bay, although I remained profoundly sceptical. Many wild tales of strange and bloodcurdling incidents on Soay were current in the glen at that time, but whenever we passed the island it always looked completely deserted and the sort of place where nothing could possibly happen. We went to Rhum on Ron Macdonald's leaky old boat, grossly overloaded nearly down to the gunwales, and ran up Askival while he waited for us on the beach. There were many sea trips over the years and he used to let the children steer the boat while he fished. He was a cheerful, friendly character always on the lookout for the 'polis' who, it was rumoured, were lying in wait to catch him, in *flagrante delicto*, for alleged breaches of assorted maritime regulations. There were no apprehensions when we were aboard but on one occasion Ron dropped us hurriedly on the shore some distance from his usual beaching place and immediately put to sea again, ostensibly because the law was on his track, but we never got to the root of the matter. And the next time we met him in the Sligachan Inn—two of us came in for much needed refreshment after completing the traverse of the Cuillin ridge—he had no information to impart and didn't seem to think there was anything interesting or unusual about doing the ridge, either. But I have very happy memories of many trips across the sea with the Skye boatman. It was rumoured you took your life in your hands when you stepped on board, but we went through some

Head of Wythburn valley

Ullswater from Arthur's Pike

Blaven and Clach Glas

pretty rough seas with Ron on occasions, and always emerged unscathed—and generally with a free catch of fish as well.

One year my brother and I went to Skye in early April and were astonished and dismayed to find the ridge plastered in snow and ice. There had been no sign of snow in Lakeland; we had been foolish enough to come without our ice-axes, intending to do some rock-climbing, and were unable to borrow any. I think this was the first and last occasion I have been on the mountains in alpine conditions without proper equipment, and the result was extremely sobering. For a week a fierce wind raked the corries and it was extremely cold. Rock-climbing was out of the question, for the rocks were glazed with ice and towards the ridge the snow, packed tight and frozen, was too hard for step-kicking. We were, therefore, reduced to modest expeditions up the lower hills and long walks round the coast, but even these proved adventurous enough. One walk to Loch Scavaig stands out in my memory as one of the most gruelling fights against the elements I have had to endure. More than once we were literally blown off our feet and there were times when we thought we would never get back. On another day we managed the ordinary tourist route up Bruach na Frithe—an exhilarating alpine expedition which at least provided us with some remarkable mountain photographs—but the toughest day of all was an attempt to ascend the familiar Sgurr Dearg by way of Coire na Banachdich. We thought we knew the mountain very well, but it was an unknown mountain that day. After tremendous effort, sometimes in snow up to our waists, we managed to reach the *bealach*, but the last stretch to the summit, which we had run up and down on several occasions, proved quite impossible without ice-axes. We got about halfway up by arduously chipping microscopic toe-holds with sharp pieces of rock, but eventually the snow and ice became too hard and polished and we had to make a delicate retreat. Perhaps this is the only occasion on record when supposedly experienced mountaineers have been beaten by the ordinary route up Sgurr Dearg, and it was with a deep sense of proper shame and frustration that we crept back down to the glen. With ice-axes and crampons, or even only with axes, we could had had some of the best winter mountaineering of our lives but, through improvidence, we had to waste the week in futile sallies. For years now there has always been an ice-axe in my car whenever I have travelled into Scotland between October and

May, and often in the Lakeland hills in winter-time I seem to be the only person with an axe strapped to his rucksack. I don't intend to be caught out again.

On several occasions I have seen golden eagles in Skye and once, from the rock turrets of Bidein Druim nan Ramh, we watched two of them sailing over the wild expanse of Harta Corrie. One summer evening I was walking along down Coire na Creiche after a walk over Sgurr a' Mhadaidh and had almost reached the track that joins the road through the glen when I saw a golden eagle perched on a rock a few yards ahead. I must have surprised him by suddenly appearing round a corner of crag and I think I saw him before he spotted me for I had a couple of seconds to study him in lordly repose before he spread out his great wings and, with a couple of slow downbeats, gradually sailed off down the glen. Many years later, when driving along the narrow road that winds along the northern shore of lonely Loch Hourn, I saw a second stationary eagle—this time perched on a fence-post. Again, I had just come round a corner and was suddenly presented with a remarkable opportunity to admire the bird at close quarters and watch his reflexes. As on the first occasion I was struck by how very slowly eagles take to the air and, again, there was the almost leisurely dipping of the great pinions, slowly once, twice, and then he was airborne above the Sound of Sleat on his way to Skye. Who knows, it could just have been the same eagle, for the sightings were only about 25 miles apart which must be a short flight for these fine birds.

But my most rewarding sighting of a golden eagle occurred when two of us were climbing the White Slab route above Coire a'Ghrunnda in the southern Cuillin. We were poised high up on the climb when we heard the rustling of wings below us, and there, perhaps 20 feet beneath our feet, was a magnificent golden eagle sailing across the face of the crag. For two or three minutes we had him under observation, sometimes looking up at him as he slowly banked and soared, but more often looking down on his tremendous wing-span as he dipped towards the corrie and then, after a final proud circle, his wing tips almost sweeping the rocks, sailed superbly over the ridge. We judged his wing-span to be seven or eight feet and the pinions, like outstretched fingers at the ends of his powerful wings, were particularly noticeable. His magnificent plumage was dark, shiny brown but much lighter, almost golden, on the back of the neck and on the leading edge of the wings. We had the feeling that he was inspecting us with some suspicion, perched, as we were, halfway up what might have been his own crag, for he swooped very close on two or three occasions before accelerating, with tremendous speed, into the next corrie.

Much of the magic of Skye comes from the sea. Although the ragged coastline must be something like 300 miles long there is no place on the island more than five miles from the sea, and from almost anywhere you can see it—often a deep Mediterranean blue, with white waves breaking on to beaches of yellow sand. From the hills of Skye or from its western coastlines you can see the nearer islands and, beyond them, the Outer Hebrides, the Uists and Harris, Barra and Benbecula and the rest, strung out along the horizon. Sixty miles further west lies the lonely island of St Kilda and west of that again is the end of the European continental shelf where the floor of the Atlantic Ocean drops down sharply to a thousand fathoms. It is the sight and the sound of the sea that provides much of the fascination of Skye. You go there for the climbing and the ridge walking, but always there are the blue waters far below, the sight of the islands and the smell of the tangle. Besides the eagles, the buzzards and the ravens there are the sea birds and even on the highest peaks you hear the screaming of the gulls and see them searching the topmost rocks for the abandoned sandwich.

They call Skye 'the Misty Isle' but this characteristic can be one of its attractions. Skye is a fairyland so close to the sea and the clouds that the scenery is changing all the time. Any moment the mists may clear—first, a tiny patch of blue in the sky, then a rocky summit suddenly looming out of the mist and then a distant splash of sun on a glistening hillside. One moment everything is wet and miserable; the next, the rocks can be steaming in the sunshine, white clouds breaking over the peaks and, far below, blue waters dancing out to the horizon. I remember one day, when the weather forecast for the north-west of Scotland was 'heavy rain', when we went up the Pinnacle Ridge of Sgurr nan Gillean and never saw a cloud or a human being all day. From the top we could see not only the whole line of the Outer Hebrides but scores of the highest mountains in Scotland from the lonely peaks of Sutherland to Ben Nevis and beyond. All the great sea lochs of the western Highlands were revealed—well-remembered places like Loch Torridon, Loch

Carron, Loch Hourn, Loch Nevis, Loch Ailort and then the great sweep out to Ardnamurchan Point. Another day we did the traverse of Blaven and Clach Glas and saw Loch Scavaig and the Atlantic below our feet and the whole line of the Cuillin ridge, thirty peaks from Gars-bheinn to Sgurr nan Gillean, stretched like a jagged saw across the setting sun.

My last memory of Skye is of one May when two of us sat on the tiny summit of Sgurr Alastair, the highest peak of the Cuillin, after a rock-climb in the sunshine up one of the steep walls that encircle Coire Lagan. Snow still clung in places to the crags and the day was so clear that we could pick out the colouring of the fields in the Outer Hebrides, and see mile after mile of snow-capped mainland peaks, looking for all the world like a corner of Switzerland. Not a breath of wind stirred the air and the smoke from our pipes floated straight up into the cloudless sky. The only sound was an occasional 'swish' as a slab of melting snow peeled off the crags and slithered into the corrie, steaming in the heat 2,000 feet below our feet.

For me and many others, Skye is still a magical place, despite all the changes of the last forty years. New roads, mass tourism and mountaineering developments have all had their impact but the great rock peaks and the lonely corries are still unchanged and the golden eagle still nests in the crags. But I can also treasure memories of ordinary, everyday, but still magical, things—the lilting, high-pitched speech and the kindliness of the islanders, the screaming of the sea birds along the coast, a line of rolling surf on a yellow beach, the stooked corn in the evening sun, the peat smoke in the evenings and, always, the sight and sound of the deep blue sea.

SEEKING THE HIGHLANDS

Years ago I used to reckon that the real Scotland, the Highlands if you like, started at about the Ballachulish Ferry, but nowadays I'm more inclined to place the gateway much further north. What many of us are seeking when we go to the Highlands is a breath of pure mountain air, untarnished by commercialization and the more tawdry aspects of tourism—the Scotland we knew forty years ago when lonely white beaches and remote blue lochans could still be 'discovered'. Today, I would say that it is not until you drive north of, say, the Garve to Ullapool road that you get through the bed-and-breakfast belt, and past the more crowded caravan sites, the roadside knick-knack shops and the bagpiper mendicants. Somewhere about this line the air seems to become clearer, the colours sharper, the hills more shapely and the distant views more extensive. The caravans are not so thick on the ground, the drivers on the narrow roads are more courteous, and the commercial flavour has almost completely disappeared. You may well see red deer from the roads or even eagles and you feel you are back in the real Highlands again. Ullapool itself has now gone in for motels, and glorious Achmelvich Bay where, years ago, we used to bathe costumeless is now a busy caravan site, but in five recent expeditions to the hills in this area I did not see one other person. They have had to take steps to prevent erosion by feet on the steep slopes of little Stac Polly, with a car-park at its foot, but the bigger, remoter mountains are just as they were thirty or forty years ago—trackless and still bare of orange peel and beer-can rings.

5

Long Days in Lakeland

Some Rewarding Permutations

Long days in the Lakeland hills are easily planned. You can walk across the district in a day, link the main passes in a circular round, keep to the ridges enclosing the longer dales, take a straight compass line, following it exactly, from one point on the map to another, or merely walk round Windermere or some other considerable lake. Another variation might be to collect all the summits in one area—the Wasdale hills, for example, can make a pretty hard day—or you can walk up Scafell the way the Victorian mountaineers used to do it, from the railway station on the coast, or tramp the whole length of High Street in the steps of the Romans. The permutations are endless, and the possibilities for enjoying fresh air, exercise and splendid scenery only limited by legs and lungs; but the long day most favoured by people who want to test their staying powers is the round of the Lakeland 'Threes'—the handful of fells exceeding 3,000 feet in height. It is not the most enjoyable mountain day that could be devised—far too much road walking is involved—but the round, although comparatively commonplace nowadays, still retains a certain cachet and its successful completion at least confirms that one is reasonably fit. A round to get out of one's system, and not often repeated, although a particularly tough friend of mine went round a second time, in bad weather, a year or two ago—as a sixty-fifth birthday gesture.

It was the Victorians who first started doing long walks in the Lakeland hills. A little more than one hundred years ago a Mr Thomas Watson of Darlington, accompanied by Wilson, the Lodore 'guide', set off from Keswick and walked over Scafell Pike in a snow storm, went on to Helvellyn in thick mist and finished up with Blencathra and Skiddaw in a strong wind that forced them to crawl over the more exposed sections on hands and knees. They then returned to their starting point, 20 hours 45 minutes after they had set out, after completing the biggest mountain walk that had ever taken place in the Lake District. They reckoned they had covered about 48 miles and climbed up and down something like 10,500 feet. Predictably, it created quite a stir, but times change. Nowadays, perhaps a hundred or more people complete a similar round—excluding Blencathra but including Scafell—every year but never even get their names in the papers. What was once a very considerable achievement has now become just a long, hard day, although the feat remains the same test of stamina. The mountains and the distances are the same, but the people are tougher, or, at least, more determined.

Much of the credit for this fairly recent increasing awareness that personal standards of physical fitness may be higher than is generally realized, that you need not necessarily be an athlete to accomplish quite significant achievements, must go to the Lake District area of the Ramblers Association. Since 1965 they have been organizing their annual marathon walk over the principal 3,000–footers of England, and, as a result, several hundred ordinary mountain folk have discovered they have inner reserves of endurance, strength and determination they had not believed possible. Eighty-four people started on the first marathon and 65 finished, and during the first nine years it has been held a total of 651 walkers have completed the round—besides, of course, many other people who, like myself, have gone round privately at other times. What I like about the Ramblers' marathon is that it is not a race and that nobody ever wins. Those who take part are not competing against others but rather, in a sense, against themselves. They are merely, I believe, making personal assessments of their own fitness and while many of them wish to get round in, say, 16 hours or so, they are not greatly concerned about other people's times. Middle-aged mountain walkers, unable to get into the hills every weekend, who get round in 20 hours or more may have achieved a personal performance just as praiseworthy, or perhaps even more so, as that of a highly trained youngster who completes the distance in 10 or 12 hours. If some people do care to run round in 10 hours or less, good luck to them; they have proved themselves in their own way.

Joss Naylor of Wasdale, about whom I have written elsewhere in this book, went round the Ramblers' marathon in 8 hours 24 minutes in 1970 and this was still the 'record' in 1973, although the organizers are more interested in a considerable number of safely-completed rounds than in fast times. Mountain safety is an important factor in this annual walk and the Association rightly insist on proper footwear and clothing.

An incident of the 1971 walk, passed on to me by my brother who happened to be coming off Helvellyn on a private walk when some of the later marathon walkers were toiling up the fell, is worth recalling. There was a little mist along the summit ridge and one of the perspiring, jaded walkers asked my brother the way—rather a surprising question to be asked on a well-marked path on the most popular mountain in England. The walker, middle-aged and very tired indeed, seemed glad to stop for a moment and admitted, remarkably, that not only had he never been on Helvellyn before but that it was his first visit to the Lake District and that his ascents that day had been his first ever on any mountains. Several thoughts about mountain safety, navigation in bad weather and so on, no doubt crossed my brother's mind but, being a kindly soul, he merely asked the man what sort of a time he had had. And the man, with no idea where he was, tired out and with something like 10 miles to go, replied simply: 'This has been the finest day of my life.' There seemed nothing more to be said. One might deplore the fact that a middle-aged man, without mountain experience of any kind, should be allowed to go wandering over the hills on one of the most strenuous mountain walks in the country, but, at the same time, there also seemed something rather fine that this ordinary townsman, stirred by some hidden impulse, had decided to tackle the marathon—to see what he had in him.

My own round was achieved when I was within a few months of my sixtieth birthday and my companion was nearly four years older, which suggests that age is not very important. Why I had waited so long, after something like forty-five years of mountain adventure, to tackle this walk I can't say, except that for many years rock-climbing always seemed more important than mountain walking. Perhaps I just wanted to get it out of my system before it was too late. We kept up our scheduled times almost to the minute, walked the roads but trotted down all the downhill sections, and even managed a sort of shambling run down the last 2 miles into Keswick.

We had left Keswick, in a light shower of rain, at two o'clock in the morning and the ascent of Skiddaw went easily enough, except that navigation was rather difficult at times in the thick mist and the continued recital of the mournful Lyke Wake Dirge by my companion, at the steepest part, didn't help matters very much. Halfway up, when we could still see the lights of Keswick through the mist, we passed five people who were hoping to see the sunrise from the summit, but must have been disappointed. The only other encounter was with a deer which we disturbed, comfortably asleep in the bracken, when we were trotting down Latrigg. The 10 miles of road to Seathwaite in mountain boots were rather trying but it was pleasant to enjoy a completely deserted Borrowdale and to breakfast leisurely at the farm, with 21 miles behind us. Scafell was reached in mist and against quite strong head winds by way of the Lingmell col, Lord's Rake and the West Wall Traverse and Scafell Pike soon afterwards. There was a curious contretemps on the top of Scafell when my companion, Ivan Waller, a well-known mountaineer who is still climbing hard rock routes, declined to approach the Pike by way of Broad Stand. Despite the fact that Ivan is often to be seen on very severe climbs he confessed he had 'a thing' about Broad Stand, unroped, and although I told him I had once got my dog down it he wasn't to be persuaded. So we had to rattle all the way down to Lord's Rake and up to Mickledore by the long way round—an extra expenditure of time and energy I had not expected.

On the Pike we met some French walkers, exchanged some desultory and slightly halting conversation, and then picked up Broad Crag and Ill Crag, two 3,000 feet summits that are not included in the Ramblers' marathon. Near Angle Tarn we met my brother who had walked over from Wythburn and accompanied us to the end of the walk. The Stake Beck was dancing in the sunshine, the mists blown away and the hardest part of the day was over. Ahead rose the ridge of High Raise and, far behind, the whaleback length of the Helvellyn plateau but we felt quite fresh, especially after we had eaten a tin of mandarin oranges. For some time we debated whether or not we should have a bathe in the beck, so delightful were the pools, but in the end we compromised with a paddle, before going over the shoulder of High Raise and down to Greenup Edge. The Wythburn bogs were quickly and unceremoniously negotiated—I was wearing a tattered pair of boots that had kept my feet cool and wet all day, so that caution was unnecessary—and we started the ascent of Helvellyn wet through, inside and out, for Eric Arnison had met us at Wythburn church with an excellent concoction, liberally laced with sherry. The four of us, with ages totalling 248 years, went over Helvellyn and Low Man in a bitingly cold wind, with nobody else about and splendid views, and Thirlspot was reached in good order, Ivan practising skiing turns on the screes as we came down the fell. After quite a hard day the inn proved an irresistible attraction and we spent some time consuming beer and discussing tactics for the remaining 6 miles of road walking, the final arrangement being that Eric should drive on ahead and further refresh us, at appropriate intervals, with libations of malt whisky. As a result of all this preoccupation with drink we reached Keswick in a slight haze—but in plenty of time before the pubs closed—after a rewarding day. Although we noted our times on the summits this was a very light-hearted, and far from serious, expedition for we stopped when we felt like it, even telephoning wives on one occasion, and wasted a lot of time on food, drink and general merriment. One strange feature of the day was that Ivan went off to sleep whenever we stopped and finished curled up on a window ledge in a Keswick street, perfectly sober but blissfully out to the world. I mostly subsisted on honey sandwiches and glucose tablets while he chewed unappetizing strips of cold, underdone steak every hour or two. We got round in 20 hours, including all stops, which is pretty slow going, but we had not been out to break any records or even to do a reasonable time but merely to have a good day out. Having had no sleep the night before I then slept the clock round, but the indefatigable Ivan was up bright and early the next morning to do another mountain walk.

Our round included all the seven 3,000 feet tops in the Lake District—the Ramblers' do the four main ones as well as High Raise which is an unnecessary addition. The walk is spoiled by 16 miles of road walking but to keep on the tops all day would mean a much harder and longer day that would probably be beyond most ordinary mountain walkers. Keswick is the traditional start of the walk but you can start it anywhere along the route. My brother has been round starting and finishing at Seathwaite which leaves the 10 miles road walk to Borrowdale to the end, and I have known people who have started from Langdale, making a more strenuous day.

A much more modest Lakeland walk, which at least lacks artificiality, is to tramp from Penrith to Windermere along the spine of High Street. It is 27 miles—many of them rather dreary—from the Cumberland town to the rail terminus at Windermere by way of Kirkstone Pass, but a much more rewarding walk, perhaps 4 miles shorter, the way the Romans went—over the mountains. They steered a bee-line route, mostly south by south-west, over the highest fells east of Kirkstone, making a mountain highway for their soldiers between their forts at Brougham and Ambleside. Their chariots and slave-borne litters went this way, along the edge of the crags that look down into a dozen lonely valleys and, through the centuries, many travellers have passed along this airy highway. Even before the Roman cohorts marched along this long backbone of the fells the ancient Britons had their settlements on the lower slopes at either end and later the Scots raiders—to be repulsed, it is said, on the Troutbeck fells—came this way. For hundreds of years shepherds and foxhunters have also known this mountain route, and at one time High Street was the scene of the annual carousels at the shepherds' meets. Somehow or other they used to drag barrels of ale to the top of the fell—more than 2,700 feet high—and at one time they even had horse-racing up there. You can still see Race-horse Hill marked on some maps. The Romans, it is thought, took to the fells because the valleys were then mostly woods and marshes, no doubt running with wolves, wild swine and other animals. It was probably easier to go over the tops than to cut down the woods and drain the marshes before they could begin to lay their road. Cornelius Nicholson who wrote *Annals of Kendal* last century believed that the Roman 'road' over High Street was 16 to 18 feet wide, the usual width of their roads, and he managed to trace part of the line which he thought had been sunk up to 2 feet, but later mostly filled in by the passage of the centuries. The sward over the road last century, Nicholson found, was of a brighter and livelier green than the rest of the fell.

But all the signs of a long and romantic history have now all disappeared and along the northern half of the 'road' there is now not even a track or a cairn to indicate where the route might have gone. True, there is the walkers' track along the spine of High Street itself but, northwards from Loadpot Hill, you have to find your own route through the bogs, steering north-east for Penrith and wishing the Romans had had the time to put down a bit of hardcore. They say there are one or two flat stones near the top of High Street which might be the remains of the Roman 'road' but I have never been able to identify them with any certainty. Nowadays, High Street—the road, not the mountain—is no more than a line on the map, marked 'Roman road, course of'. You have just got to accept that this is the way the legions went and, if you have any imagination at all, be amazed at the boldness and wonder of it all.

The last time I went this way, in June 1972, the idea was to fit in a pleasant walk over the tops from Penrith to Windermere and get nicely sun-tanned in the process. The weather the previous day was perfect, there was a promising sunset and the weather report was favourable. We would walk south from Penrith, with the sun in our faces the whole way, and although some of the walk might be rather commonplace there would, at least, be magnificent views from the heights. But the situation the following morning proved rather different and once again underlined my slightly jaundiced opinion that to expect the exact opposite of the televised weather forecast is a reasonable guide for the Lakeland hills. It was, of course, raining, the clouds were down, in a thick grey shroud, to about 1,000 feet and much worse was to come, for when we started on the walk we found we had to contend with strong head-on winds that remained, full in our faces, all that long, wet day. Two of us left our car at Windermere and proceeded, in a friend's car, towards Penrith, but the weather looked so frightful that, a mile or two south of the town, near Tirril, we got out to start our walk, preferring to eschew the lanes around the motorway. By the time we reached Celleron the rain had increased to a downpour and we were getting buffeted by the wind that was to increase to something approaching gale force on the heights. Near Winder Hall where we took to the fell, through sodden, tussocky grass, we saw a farm-hand, who gave us a pitying glance, and he was the last human being we saw that day until we reached the outskirts of Windermere. Visibility throughout, once we had gained a little height, was down to a few yards and we had to steer by compass much of the way. Before we climbed into the mists we saw a stone circle, several tumuli and other evidences of lost civilization, and on the slopes of Arthur's Pike we saw fell ponies and put up a mountain hare that set off towards Helton as if he'd seen ghosts. On the way up Loadpot Hill, wet through and battered by the wind, we found a hollow where we crouched, trying to convince ourselves that we were slightly sheltered from the gale, and ate some sodden sandwiches. We were particularly anxious to hit off the chimney near Loadpot Hill—all that remains of the former shooting lodge of Lowther House—to take a compass bearing, but this proved distinctly difficult, and we lost some time before we found it in thick cloud. The going now became more straightforward for we were on a track but we had to remember the distinct change of direction near Rampsgill Head which you hardly notice in fine weather. Memories of the route don't help a great deal when all you can see is a little circle of wet grass and you have to decide whether you are on High Raise, Kidsty Pike, Rampsgill Head or The Knott, but we sorted it out without much difficulty and pressed on to High Street.

Here, we thought, we were on perfectly familiar ground so we rattled on without bothering to consult the compass, making for the line of the Scots' Rake down to Troutbeck Park. But it didn't quite work out that way. After descending a few hundred feet through the cloud in what we thought was the right direction we found ourselves on craggy ground and immediately realized we were off course. Our assumption was that we must be descending the side of Thornthwaite Crag but we decided that, if this was so and we did not hit off Threshthwaite Mouth, we might find ourselves down in Pasture Beck or the Hayeswater valley by mistake. So, because we could not be sure we had turned off too soon for the Scots' Rake, we felt we had no alternative but to scramble back up the fell, reach a recognizable feature and then work things out properly. This we did but the re-ascent of the fell after a tiring day, exhausted by the wind and wet through to the skin, was annoying, and we cursed ourselves for being so casual and careless. If it had not happened to me I would have doubted whether anybody could possibly get lost on High Street, but, with nearly 100 years' experience of the Lakeland fells between us we just had to swallow our pride. How easy, after this, to realize why inexperienced people so often get lost in the hills in bad weather. We soon corrected our mistake—when we got below the mist we could see we must, indeed, have been on Thornthwaite Crag—and soon afterwards we were splashing our way down the fell towards Troutbeck Park. There were floods down in the lane but an hour or so later we could see the lights of Windermere glowing through the gloom and in a short time had found an inn with a warm fire and a pleasantly lit bar. This was one of our wettest days on the Lakeland fells, although I have known worse in Scotland. We had traversed the whole length of the Roman way and had seen nothing but, in a strange sort of way, we had had a good day. Even the worst days on the hills are enjoyable in retrospect, particularly when your legs are steaming nicely in front of a roaring fire and a nice drop of something is finding its way into the right places.

Our first longish walk, about forty-five years ago, was meant to be from Foxfield railway station to Wasdale Head, carrying tents and blankets—we didn't possess sleeping bags in those days. But our packs proved heavy for youngsters and we stopped the night in Eskdale, holding down a flapping tent in half a gale. A few years later we regularly walked from Coniston to Wasdale, by way of Walna Scar and the track over the shoulder of Harter Fell and, more than once, finished the walk in the opposite direction in darkness, including on one occasion a desperate crossing of the Duddon stepping stones with the river in spate. But our first really long day, repeated several times, was to walk from Coniston to Scafell Pike or Great Gable and back, our usual route being by way of Fell Foot, Blea Tarn, Mickleden and Rossett Gill. Almost invariably these tiring days ended with a race to catch the last train out of Coniston and I have blurred memories of trying to run, in climbing boots, from the Yewdale road end and finally sinking, completely exhausted, into the horsehair seats of a train that was already leaving the station. On another of these mountain expeditions from Coniston we encountered, somewhere near Fell Foot, what must have been a cloudburst—of such intensity that for the rest of our lives, in our private circle, a particularly wet day, when you feel you have been ducked in a river, is always referred to as a 'Fell Footer', and violent precipitations are measured as being greater or less than Fell Foot. In these years we were spending every weekend in our wooden hut at Coniston Old Hall, climbing the crags. We were not really interested in long walks but were prepared to do them to reach distant crags or, as a bit of adventure, in bad weather. Once we did the Coniston to Great Gable walk at night—in winter.

But it was many years before longish mountain walks, not involving any rock-climbing, had much attraction, and at least ten years after my first ascent of Pillar Rock—by way of Central Jordan—before I reached the top of Pillar. A long time afterwards we heard about a man who had done a series of rock-climbs in a long walk over different mountains—Pillar, the Napes and Scafell, for instance—and this, in a modest round, might have suited us, but we never thought of it. One early walk, however, with a companion who was not a climber, took us all round the Buttermere fells on both sides of the valley with the Fish Hotel nicely in between. And it was on the long slog over Buttermere Moss, on the way up Robinson, with five peaks behind us and three still to come, that I first realized the remarkable healing powers of perspiration after a lengthy session of best bitter, served, in those days, in beautiful earthenware tankards. This circuit of Buttermere, taking in eight tops, is an example of one of the great joys of fell-walking, the horseshoe rounds of Lakeland, although we perhaps did it the wrong way, starting and finishing on Honister Pass with the temptation of the Fish in between, instead of starting from Buttermere. If you glance at the Ordnance Survey's excellent tourist map of the Lake District you will see that most of its mountains are protuberances on ridges radiating from a centre—Wordsworth likened them to the spokes of a wheel—and, indeed, opportunities for these horseshoe rounds of the fells abound in Lakeland to a greater degree than in any other mountain districts in Britain. The ideal mountain walk avoids covering the same ground twice and by circling the head of a dale, with the ascent of all the summits around the skyline, the walker achieves this, keeps on the top nearly all the time and enjoys constantly changing panoramas. You can so arrange your walk—if you make it rather long or take your time over it—that you are facing the sunshine all day. Probably the best-known of these walks are the Fairfield horseshoe and the Mosedale horseshoe, the latter being the more demanding. There was even a television play written about this one although the party, I seem to remember, failed to get round.

Most people take about five hours on the Fairfield horseshoe, although some, savouring the views, take rather longer and a few, with picnicking and photography, spin it out into a long day. Going pretty steadily, without stopping, and trotting down the steep bits I have gone round in three hours from Rydal, but runners take about an hour and a half and the record—for there's an annual race around the skyline—stood at eight and a half minutes over the hour in 1973. One year I bought a pair of new boots in Ambleside and then immediately went round the Fairfield horseshoe to break them in. I was testing out a new theory which involved covering a few miles with the boots loosely fastened and then filling them with water and tying them up as tightly as possible. The immersion was achieved at the end of the round, with only a mile to go, by standing in the Rydal Beck up to knees but I finished in some discomfort and do not commend this procedure. A more recent round, in old, comfortable boots, took place on a perfect autumn day when the ridge was almost as thickly populated as Striding Edge on a summer Sunday. Everybody seemed to be going round, purposeful-striding young folk, older walkers with sticks, children in sandals, a baby strapped to a frame rucksack, and several dogs. From the tops—eight are traversed on this simple walk—I counted nearly a hundred mountains from Ingleborough to the Scafells, with a peep at the Border hills, and found Great Gable, with its massive, square-cut dome, easily the most distinctive. The graceful, triangular peak of Bowfell, the sharp prow of Kidsty Pike and the towering bulk of Pillar were almost immediately recognizable, but the deeply-scooped coves of Helvellyn, showed by the setting sun, and the dark crags of Deepdale, were more dramatic. Easdale Tarn, hidden from the sun, looked a lonely, sombre pool, but Rydal Water, mirroring its islands and a wealth of woodland, glowed like a jewel in a perfect setting. The late afternoon sunshine burnished miles of sea and coastline, danced on the waterfalls in Scandale Beck, silvered the length of Coniston Water and made the yachts on Windermere look like butterflies on a pond. The bracken slopes on Seat Sandal glowed like a russet carpet, the Rydal Hall woods were a tumult of October colour and, down the zigzags to the dale, late visitors were paying their 20 pence—plus VAT—to look through the poet's home. It must have looked much the same in Wordsworth's time—the ancient trees, the sunlight on the old stone walls, the smoke rising from cottage chimneys, the sheepdogs in the drive and the blue hills going to sleep. Only the television aerials and the car-park were new.

The last time I went round the Mosedale horsehoe was on an extremely hot summer's day—too hot for most people, perhaps, for we had the round almost to ourselves. I remember the sight of the lowland hills across the Solway from the top of Pillar and the Liza threading through the forests nearly 3,000 feet below, a wisp of cloud caught on the top of Scafell 5 miles away and, once again, the bulk of Great Gable, this time looking curiously like an atomic explosion, peeping over the top of Kirk Fell. We perched on the cairn of Red Pike, legs dangling over the crags, eating raisins and

A Scottish cornice

Sail Ghorm on Quinag

Sail Gharbh from Quinag

trying to work out a scrambling route from the corrie to the cairn, keeping on rock all the way, and we walked on to Steeple for a peep down the length of Ennerdale. Without wasting much time we got round in about six hours and decided afterwards that the most rewarding moment had been to reach the summit of Kirk Fell in the early evening and suddenly see, far below, the whole length of Wastwater beneath its shadowed crags stretching out towards the sea and the setting sun. We could see the whitewashed hotel, on the edge of the pattern of stone-walled fields, and knew that all we had to do was to trot down the steep grass and scree for the supreme delight, on such a hot day, of cool beer in a low-raftered room. I remember, at the foot of the fell, that we debated whether first to take a quick dip in the Mosedale Beck which, after some hours without sight or sound of nearby water, looked particularly enticing—but the beer won.

The Mosedale horseshoe takes in some of the most dramatic scenery in Lakeland, especially along the Pillar skyline, but the round of the Wasdale fells provides views just as magnificent, and makes a demanding day, even for a strong walker. This circuit may be varied but the usual round is from Wasdale Head over the summits of Kirk Fell, Great Gable, Great End, Scafell Pike and Scafell—some of the finest mountains in England. Some years ago an annual race over the Ennerdale horseshoe, with Green Gable as the turning point, was introduced into the runners' calendar and, more recently, runners have been going round the Wasdale hills, but, perhaps, seeing very little of the scenery. Langdale is another valley that is now attracting the long-distance runners but this should not deter walkers who wish to savour the joys of keeping on the ridges, without retracing their steps. A favourite Langdale round is the circuit of Oxendale, taking in The Band and Bowfell on one side and Crinkle Crags, Shelter Crags and Pike o' Blisco on the other. Enclosed within this round are the wild ravines of Oxendale into which one may descend at will—either for the bathing or the scrambling. A longer Langdale circuit includes the Langdale Pikes, missing out the easy approach to The Band, and reaching Bowfell by way of the top of Stake Pass, Angle Tarn and Ore Gap or over Rossett Pike. This longer walk can easily be shortened at the other end by excluding Pike o' Blisco and descending straight into Oxendale from Crinkle Crags, and another of many possible alternatives is to approach Bowfell from the top of Rossett Gill and along the climbers' track underneath Bowfell Buttress.

Many of these horseshoe rounds are particularly superb in winter—provided one has extra food and clothing, torch, whistle and ice-axe and, if there is any likelihood of ice, crampons. Two of us did the long Langdale round one December day, when the whole of Lakeland, white with new snow, stretched below us, the sun shone down out of a bright blue sky, and the distances seemed to have shrunk overnight. From the ice-covered summit rocks of Bowfell we felt we could almost throw a stone against the black Scafell crags, 2 miles away across the white wilderness of upper Eskdale, while the nuclear power-station on the Cumberland coast and the brown plantations under Skiddaw seemed only short walks away. Flat-topped Ingleborough and the other Yorkshire fells were very clear, Criffel in the Scottish lowlands easily recognized through a gap between Skiddaw and the Derwent Fells and beyond, apparently hanging from the clouds above the farthest horizon were some of the Highland peaks, looking like a distant Himalayan range. The sun was setting like a hanging curtain of gold as we crunched across the frozen surfaces of the Three Tarns and along the splintered tops of Crinkle Crags. And just before it sank out of sight behind the Wasdale hills we saw the after-glow caught on the rock turrets of the Langdale Pikes, making these modest fells soar like dolomite spires lit by an alpine dawn or summer lightning.

There are several fine horseshoe rounds in northern Lakeland, one of them starting and finishing at Braithwaite and embracing the Coledale fells with the Causey Pike range to the south and the ridge of Grisedale Pike to the north. Grasmoor can be included, if desired, and another rewarding little round embraces that mountain as well as the Hopegill Head—Whiteside ridge. This is the circuit of Gasgale Gill and can include, at the start, for rock scramblers, the ascent of the rocky front of Grasmoor that overlooks the northern end of Crummock Water. And you finish this short day, if you are lucky with the weather, by trotting down Whiteside right into the setting sun with long shadows across the meadows at Lanthwaite Green, the sunlight sparkling on Crummock Water and the bulk of Mellbreak turning purple in the evening. Buttermere, for me, is always a wonderful place either for starting or finishing a mountain walk, and W. G. Collingwood, writing more than seventy years ago, expressed the perfection of the dale better than I could ever hope to do. 'But I always think of this valley,' he wrote, 'as made by Heaven for summer evenings and summer mornings: green floor and purple heights, with the sound of waters under the sunset, or lit with the low north-eastern sun into pure colour above, and the greyness of the dew upon the grass.'

Neither Skiddaw nor Blencathra lend themselves to horseshoe rounds, except that you can easily go up one ridge and down another. But the traverse of both mountains and Lonscale Fell can make a good day—especially on skis—and circuits in unusual country can be devised at the 'back o' Skidda' where the miles can be very long. Another good winter walk or ski tour is the round of the Dodds with Hartside, while the Helvellyn range provides some magnificent short circuits around the coves and corries lying to the east of the main ridge. The familiar Striding Edge–Helvellyn–Swirrel Edge round is a miniature horseshoe and there are fine circular walks around the Kentmere fells, above the head of Mardale and along the heights circling the red deer country around Martindale. On a recent autumn walk round the tops above Ramsgill Beck I was startled to hear what sounded like a motorcycle or a car being violently 'revved-up' not far away. Since I was 4 or 5 miles away from roads I was at a loss to understand this until my eyes caught a movement in the valley far below, and I saw a red stag picking his way down the screes and roaring his defiance as he went.

The hills I know best are the Coniston fells. For years we were there nearly every weekend, mostly for the climbing on Dow Crag, but there have been dozens of occasions, right up to today, when a walk along the familiar ridges, covering all the tops, has proved just as pleasant as the first visit in the 1920s. Just over a week ago, as I write this chapter in the autumn of 1973, I did the complete round once again—Wetherlam, Greyfriar, Coniston Old Man, Dow Crag, the ridge down to Walna Scar and all the tops in between—and although I knew every yard of the way, there were new things to discover. Little things like a new cairn, the sunlight picking out a remote tarn, a forgotten feature of old mine workings, the identity of a shoulder of fell peeping over a distant ridge or just a quiet resolve to have a look some time at a likely-looking rock face underneath the summit of Great Carrs. There are ten summits on this round and it's not a hard day to go over them all, either way round, with easy walking most of the way along the broad ridges with changing views of mountains and sea, shadowed combes and lonely tarns, the swifts swooping above the Dow Crag gullies and the Herdwicks on their little trods across the screes. In winter the round is even more rewarding, but I remember one day in the early 1930s when five of us were nearly defeated on the ordinary ascent of Coniston Old Man by the familiar mines track. There was more snow on the mountain that winter than I can ever remember, so deep that the huge cairn on the summit, in those days a particularly massive affair, was completely hidden. Further complications were that the clouds were almost down to the intake fields, there was a furious gale blowing and it was snowing hard. Low Water, piled high with ice-floes, was barely recognizable, all the quarry buildings were buried beneath the snow, and we had to steer a compass course to find the summit. And when we got down to our hut at Coniston Old Hall we stood our jackets and trousers, frozen stiff as boards, in a corner and took photographs of them.

People unfamiliar with the district should remember that on a horseshoe walk you are going right round the compass so that navigation, especially in mist, can sometimes be difficult. It is a good idea, particularly if you are not familiar with the terrain, to jot down the compass bearings of the various summits from one another, so that you can adjust your course in mist, as you go round. When the walker is properly equipped the horseshoe walks of Lakeland, summer or winter, can provide many memorable days, with new ground along every yard and the sun—when you are lucky—chasing you round the clock.

But few of these horseshoe rounds—and a glance at the map will show you many more—make really long days, although, with a little ingenuity, two or three can be joined together. The longer walks follow the ridges in roughly straight lines which means you need transport at each end, but this can generally be easily arranged. A good example of this is to walk from Threlkeld to Ambleside by way of the Dodds, the Helvellyn range and the western half of the Fairfield horseshoe which makes a particularly rewarding day, especially in winter-time. This is one of the main spines of the Lake District and the going is easy all the way; I once tried to do the whole length on skis but only managed half of it. Another shorter spinal traverse, boggy in its middle section, is to walk from Keswick to Langdale over the Armboth fells, Ullscarf and the High Raise plateau, finishing with the descent of Harrison Stickle—a walk that improves in dramatic quality the further you go. Really ambitious pedestrians can walk right across the Lake District from east to west—the permutations are legion—and the more mountains you put in the more strenuous the expedition.

A refinement of this is to draw a line with a ruler right across the map and then walk along it, steering by compass and taking the ups and downs exactly as they come. One such walk was accomplished in the 1960s by Albert Riding and R. B. Evans—a walk right across the Lake District along grid 09 on the one-inch Ordnance Survey map. Having decided to walk across the district on a grid line they searched the map and found that only the 09 presented them with a dry crossing, lakes proving impassable barriers—unless they were swum—to most horizontal traverses. The walk started in Wasdale—the Westmorland Wasdale near to Shap granite quarries—and finished in the mountaineers' Wasdale—a distance of 23½ miles, involving a total ascent of about 13,000 feet. They steered by compass all the way, keeping exactly to the grid-line, but allowed themselves a little flexibility to avoid the worst of the bogs and to zigzag gently on the steep bits. The walk took them across Shap Fells, over Adam Seat, The Knowe and Froswick, down to Kirkstone Pass, over Red Screes, High Pike, Helm Crag, and Sergeant Man, down into Langstrath and over Allen Crags and the side of Great End to the finish at Wastwater Hotel. They did the walk in two sections, camping overnight near Grasmere, and found it strenuous enough with many steep sections that the ordinary fell-walker would normally circumvent. There were some craggy places, too, and a lot of unpleasant bracken, but the walk went well and, for the first 10 miles, they did not meet anybody else, although it was the height of summer. For most of the time, since paths were completely avoided, they found themselves in 'new country' although in a familiar area, and the walk had an exploratory feeling about it not experienced on a straightforward walk over the tops. But it is not necessary to cross the Lake District to achieve a demanding exercise; much shorter sections, taken along a strictly straight line, can be rewarding enough. In preparation for a more ambitious bee-line route I once walked north-west from Cockley Beck to the summit of Scafell Pike along a completely straight line and found it quite demanding. Seathwaite - Scafell Pike - Pillar and back to Seathwaite on exact bearings would, I suggest, make a strenuous triangle and the armchair walker can work out many more. Other good mountain days can be won—and I have done a lot of this—by keeping to the becks;

rock-climbing ability may be required and soakings should be expected. The amount of 'new' country that can be discovered in this way is remarkable.

As a change from the often-crowded Lakeland fells the walker can explore the Howgills, once part of Yorkshire but now within the new county of Cumbria—glorious, unspoiled country of smooth, steep-sided fells, the home of sheep, buzzards and larks but no people, except round the edges. You can walk across the Howgills in an afternoon, but for a longer expedition of 12 miles or more it is worth while, first, to go over the Tebay and Langdale fells, crossing the former county boundary about halfway along the walk. Often you will see nobody all day but, at Bank Holiday time, you might meet a few at the Sedbergh end. There will probably, however, be plenty of fell ponies, their long tails almost sweeping the ground as they placidly graze around the 2,000 feet contour. The Howgills sheep, black-faced Rough Fells, are different from our Lake District mountain sheep that scatter as you approach—even the patient, grey-faced Herdwicks that, otherwise, seem to be possessed of remarkable, long-suffering resignation. But the sheep you meet on the Howgills walk up to inspect you, not being used to human beings, while the larks accompany you in season, singing overhead. If you take a zigzag line on this walk from Tebay, seeking out all the fells on the horizon, you can pick up fourteen tops, but only at the southern end of the walk are there any tracks. You find your own way through a confusion of fells, all shaped alike, and separated by nearly a score of valleys, often unvisited for months. There are no cairns to trip over, no orange peel or empty beer cans and only, for the first few miles, the distant sound of the motorway to remind you that civilization is not far away. Otherwise, just sunlit fells, sweeping depths below your feet and views across half of England. Halfway along the walk you cross Carlin Gill, a fine dog-leg ravine, and for a shorter, although more strenuous, expedition you can follow the ravine from the lovely Fair Mile road above the Lune, scramble up Black Force, finishing with a rock route at the top, and come down Cautley Spout to the Kirkby Stephen road. And to make this shorter walk into a worthwhile day—and avoid the use of a second car—you can come back the same way. If the Howgills were a few hundred feet higher they would provide the best skiing country in England. As it is I have often skied there on my own on perfect, sunlit snow, unmarked by anybody else, when hundreds of skiers have been crowding the popular runs on Raise and Great Dun Fell. The Howgills are an extra reward for living in southern Lakeland. I can see them from my windows—a long line of sleek summits in this view although, in reality, a considerable triangle of fells—and I go there when the roads into the Lakes are chock-full of traffic and I want to find somewhere to think.

Sometimes, at Bank Holiday time, we escape into Yorkshire and at the end of these days on lonely, limestone fells where the miles seem to leap away to incredibly distant horizons, it is pleasant to drive home at speed on a traffic-free width of road, while cars travelling south and east away from the Lake District are crawling, bumper to bumper, towards the towns. Ingleborough is a familiar sight from the Lakeland Hills and a rewarding little hill. Elsewhere, I refer to the Three Peaks race—Ingleborough, Whernside and Pen-y-Ghent—which, for ordinary people like myself, makes a long day. The record for this round, taken at the run, is an incredible $2\frac{1}{2}$ hours or so, but the first time my brother and I walked round, without noticeably wasting time, we took about nine hours. This seemed ridiculous and I privately decided that I really ought to be able to get round in eight hours—even in heavy boots and carrying a rucksack. A year or two ago, when I was in my sixties, I had the opportunity to try to recover my self-esteem, for a walk was organized for elderly Rotarians and I was entered. This was not quite the traditional Three Peaks round for the start was at Dale Head and the finish at Clapham but the mileage was only fractionally less. Although this was not a race—it was a sponsored walk and you made money for a good cause even if you did one of the three summits—some of us took it fairly seriously. I had expected most of the huge field of over 250 to be as elderly as myself, but the entrants included several younger men, including youngsters clearly out to show us how to do it. In the event I finished in the first half dozen or so, in just over seven hours, but any satisfaction I may have felt was dampened by the fact that two of the entrants who finished well ahead of me were both several years older than myself. Most people went round sensibly, taking their time—in some cases, twelve hours or more—and enjoying the scenery; only a few hot-heads like myself, trying to convince themselves they were not as feeble as they looked and felt, went as hard as they could go. But even the performances of those of us who finished in reasonable time proved the extent of the vast gulf that separates mountain walkers who think they are fairly fit from runners who know they are.

My passable performance was largely achieved by guile and gamesmanship, although I was handicapped by officialdom and boots that were far too stiff and heavy. We were taken to the start in buses and I took care to get in the first one with the result that I reached the top of Pen-y-Ghent in the first ten. Feeling fairly fresh I then started running, thus achieving an element of surprise, for elderly Rotarians don't normally run down mountains, so that I reached Ribblehead—knowing the route—before anybody else. I then made the mistake of asking the way, not because I didn't know it but because I had been told we had to follow a special route and not just any old way, and was directed along the railway line for a mile or two. This was not the route I had planned for Whernside and I later had the mortification, on the roundabout ascent to the summit I had been told to take, of seeing later competitors taking the direct route from which I had been debarred. In this way, through doing as I was told instead of keeping my mouth shut like the others, I had lost my lead by the time I reached the summit, and never regained it, although I tried hard enough. In fact, I never saw any more competitors, either ahead of me or behind, until I reached Clapham, which just shows how the broad acres of Yorkshire can swallow up human beings.

This was a good, longish day and a lonely one, which seemed surprising since so many of us were involved. The official route was much more roundabout in several places than the one I had planned —it took us, for instance, to Hull Pot, although there is a much shorter alternative. We had good weather, the mists on the fell tops rising as we approached, and the distant views over most of Yorkshire were superb. In bad weather, which I have never experienced on the Three Peaks, the round, I'm sure, can be confusing if you do not know the route. It can also be extremely boggy and decidedly slippery, if you are running the downhill sections. The initial pull up Pen-y-Ghent is pleasant and straightforward, and the run down easy, but the subsequent route-finding to Ribblehead can be rather confusing—particularly if there is a bull in one of the fields, as there was on one of my rounds. Whernside is rather tiring and tussocky and the final slope just below the summit one of the steepest in the district, but the descent to Hill Inn can be run all the way, if you still feel fresh. I found the ascent of Ingleborough, on my last round, something of a slog but, from the summit, it was a relief to pick out Gaping Gill in the distance and to know that it was now downhill all the way. In several ways, apart from the route, this sponsored walk was not the usual Three Peaks round. We finished up at Giggleswick school where we had showers and then the headmaster kindly allowed us the use of the school swimming bath, which was invigoratingly cold. But one of the great moments of my day came a little later when I stopped at a farmhouse with a sign 'Teas'. The farmer's wife was pleasant and chatty and, in a cool little parlour looking out on a pretty rose garden, served tea in a huge earthenware pot. And I had six steaming cups and, had I had the nerve, would have asked for more.

THE HEART OF LAKELAND

The twin, sharply scooped valleys of Easdale, dropping steeply eastwards in green shelves and craggy steps from the great central plateau of High Raise, provide the ideal walk on a winter's afternoon. There is something of an unchanging, almost primeval, atmosphere about these lonely dales, for you can see how the ice has sculptured the corries and dammed up the tarns, and, once past the intake fields, you are looking at a tumbled landscape that was just the same before the dawn of history. You can wander up a quiet Grasmere lane, stroll past the lovely houses so perfectly sited under the steeps of Helm Crag and be standing atop the lofty hub of the Lake District in a little over an hour. Draw a circle of perhaps 15 miles radius centred on High Raise and you include all the mountains, and if you stand by the cairn you can see nearly all of them crowded, distantly, on every horizon. Here, surely, is the perfect upland promenade, the real centre of the National Park, as flat as a Derbyshire moorland but girt on all sides by unseen depths. It was still and close the other day by the waterfalls in Far Easdale Gill under the crags of Deer Bield but on High Raise the wind was bitter and the frozen turf and clumps of staghorn moss covered in a white mantle of hoar frost. Codale Tarn lay dark and forbidding in the shadows of Sergeant Man and you could see how aeons ago the ice must have piled up its scouring and blocked the outlet from the corrie to form this lovely pool. On the next shelf lower down slumbered Easdale Tarn itself—a smooth, black mirror circled by holly trees in a silence so complete you could have heard the insects talking. And lower down the jackdaws had gone to sleep by Kitty Crag and the first lights were yellowing the dusk under Helm Crag.

6

Record Walks and Runs

Towards the Limit of Endurance

One bright August day in the curiously mixed summer of 1973 when we had droughts, thunderstorms, floods and long, sunny days of cloudless skies, two of us went up Yewbarrow from Wasdale Head, straight up the fell from the bridge over the Mosedale Beck. It was very hot, we had fairly bulky rucksacks and the ground was unmitigatingly steep, trackless and rough, consisting of sliding scree and stony bracken, bilberry, heather and grass. It was impossible to maintain any sort of rhythm, so cunningly were the boulders concealed in the bracken and so unstable the screes, and the perspiration ran into our eyes and off the ends of our noses. There are not many steeper and rougher slopes in the Lake District and when, with aching calf muscles, we reached the cairn in just over the hour, we decided we had not done too badly. It was now even hotter and Wastwater, far below, with the sunlight on the water, looked temptingly inviting but we turned right and carried on round the Mosedale horseshoe, covering Red Pike, Scoat Fell, Steeple and Pillar, and then adding Kirk Fell, with its steep scramble from Black Sail and its headlong descent of grass and scree, because this has always seemed to us the logical conclusion to the round. With a short stop for lunch and one or two pauses to admire the view or to soak up perspiration with sodden handkerchiefs we got round in about six hours, and the beer at the Wastwater Hotel has rarely tasted better.

I only mention this very modest round, which is certainly nothing to crow about, to try to put into some sort of perspective the achievements of this twentieth-century breed of supermen who run up and down mountains, instead of walking over them, and try to do as many as possible in the quickest time they can manage. Certainly, they've no time to look at the scenery or to savour the character of the hills, being far too busy placing their nimbly dancing feet or consulting their watches, but they must form part of my story for almost every one I have met—and I know dozens of them—has a real affection for mountains, although seeming to treat them so cavalierly, and all have more experience of long days in the hills than most of us. And the fitness and endurance of the breed are quite exceptional. Let me quote an example. A few weeks before my brother and I last ambled round the Mosedale horseshoe in August 1973 two of the best-known of these long-distance fell-runners, Alan Heaton and Joss Naylor, went over the same ground. I watched them from the Brackenclose woods and noted that they disappeared over the top of the exasperatingly steep fellside beyond the Mosedale Beck in exactly 25 minutes which means that they would have reached the cairn, invisible from the dale, in about half an hour or less. It had taken my brother and I, you will remember, just over the hour, although, of course, we were not racing and were wearing boots and carrying rucksacks. In addition, we were both in our sixties, although pretty fit and used to long, mountain days, but Heaton and Naylor are not youngsters either, one being in his forties and the other approaching them.

But it is the subsequent part of the day that is significant and interesting. We got over our sixth peak, Kirk Fell, and down to Wasdale in about 6 hours from the start; Heaton and Naylor carried on over Great Gable, Base Brown, Brandreth and Grey Knotts and down to Honister Pass, where we were waiting to feed them with fruit drinks and glucose, in 3 hours from Wasdale. Naylor then trotted back to Wasdale, over part of the way he had come, to milk his cows, while Heaton carried on for another 15 hours or more over another thirty-eight mountains, all through that day and throughout the night, only retiring when the onset of bad weather made his chances of completing a record round remote. He had been trying to improve on Naylor's fantastic round the year before of no fewer than sixty-three Lakeland peaks traversed within 24 hours which represents a distance of 92 miles and an ascent and descent of 35,000 feet—up and down Everest, if you like, with another 6,000 feet tacked on. With this sort of day ahead of him—and he was trying to put in even more summits—you might have thought that Heaton would have treated Yewbarrow, his first peak, with more respect, and perhaps conserved his energies a little on his initial traverse of the Wasdale fells. But the pair of them arrived at Honister as if they had just been for a gentle walk over Great Gable, although they had been over eleven summits in half the time we had taken to go over six. We were pleasantly tired at the end of the day and ready to relax over a couple of pints of beer. Heaton was perhaps only a sixth of his way round and had more than fifty peaks ahead of him. But at least he agreed that the ascent of Yewbarrow direct from Wasdale Head is a discouraging start to any day, whether you plan to do six mountains or sixty. 'I always reckon I'm halfway round when I get to the top of Yewbarrow,' he joked. 'It's the first one you do and the worst, and I generally go up in a sort of daze.'

Alan Heaton, a rather stocky Lancastrian, looks a fairly ordinary sort of chap but is possessed of quite extraordinary determination as well as having remarkable fitness and staying power. He was the first man to improve on the Lakeland 24 hours fell record set up by the late Bob Graham—forty-two summits during the day—after it had stood unequalled, despite many attempts, for twenty-eight years. In an earlier book, published in 1963,* I traced the history of this unique challenge, starting with its very earliest beginnings, more than 100 years ago, when people first began to tackle really big walks in the hills, and finishing with Heaton's performance, in August 1962, when he notched up fifty-four peaks within the day. After his first breakthrough, two years earlier, when he had completed Bob Graham's round, Heaton's feat had been bettered by his older brother Kenneth who had done a round of fifty-one peaks, but the following year Alan recaptured the record. But as the book was going to press there came an even more remarkable round—fifty-six Lakeland mountains in 23 hours 35 minutes—put up by, in some ways, an even more remarkable man, the late Eric Beard of Leeds, whose various achievements I discuss later in this chapter. Eric appeared almost out of the blue and, with no previous knowledge of parts of the round but favoured by good weather, he managed to improve slightly on Alan Heaton's round—largely on a diet of 'jam butties'. We were to hear a great deal more about this single-minded personality during his remaining six years of life, but

* *In Mountain Lakeland* (Guardian Press).

in the meantime his achievement suggested that a round of sixty Lakeland peaks within the day might be a possibility.

It was in July 1965 that this phenomenal feat was achieved, and the runner was again the extraordinary Alan Heaton. This time he started from the Old Dungeon Ghyll Hotel in Langdale, met mist and rain on Great Gable, and mist on Skiddaw and on the Dodds where he had a bad time, hearing what he thought were cow-bells and imagining he was in the Alps. Runners sometimes get a little light-headed after many hours of great exertion, but the 'cow bells' turned out to be the whistle and compass of one of his companions clanging together, and Alan quickly recovered. Apart from an encounter with midges on the Langdale Pikes he had no further trouble, and completed his round in just over 23 hours. This record, many of us considered, would surely represent the ultimate of human endurance and, indeed, it stood for six years, but in June 1971 it was beaten, although narrowly, by a man who was born in the fells and had spent his life among them—Joss Naylor, a sheep farmer who lives at the foot of Yewbarrow in Wasdale. Once again, the old tradition of the holder of the record assisting the contender was employed, Alan Heaton accompanying Naylor along several sections of the route. Naylor started from his home at Wasdale Head, his first fell being the rough, steep slopes of Yewbarrow which he probably knows better than anybody else, but the start was delayed for an hour because of low clouds, rain and high winds. This weather was to continue for much of the day and wet and greasy rock slowed him down at times but he added Base Brown and Causey Pike to Heaton's total of peaks—although missing out Lingmell—and got round in 23 minutes under the 24 hours. This was a remarkable round for although he had only covered marginally more ground than Alan Heaton had done he had had to contend, in his sixty-one peaks, with very poor conditions.

But Naylor could not be completely satisfied with his performance, holding the record by such a narrow margin, and decided to try to improve on it the following year. Again he started from Wasdale Head, reaching the top of Yewbarrow in the fantastic time of 25 minutes, but, again, he was to be hampered throughout by thick cloud and, later, heavy rain. Almost every summit was in cloud, the moon which he had hoped would assist him over the Dodds was blotted out, and when he reached Grisedale Tarn, after traversing the Helvellyn range, he decided against attempting Fairfield,

Greatrigg Man and Hart Crag. He had earlier, however, added Whiteless Pike in the Grasmoor group to his total of summits but the thick mist and heavy rain on the Langdale fells made the going very difficult, with torches in use all the time, and the cairn on Sergeant Man proving particularly elusive. But once he was in the Scafells he was on the home stretch and, despite the continued heavy rain, strong winds and thick cloud, Naylor, with his last trio of companions, trotted over the rocky summits, added Lingmell to his total of the year before, and ran down to Brackenclose in appalling weather, drenched to the skin but by no means exhausted, and a very happy man. He had completed a circuit of sixty-three Lakeland peaks in 23 hours 35 minutes on one of the worst days that could be imagined—the biggest 'walk' in the fells that anybody had ever done in one day. Measured on the map it works out at about 92 miles—something like the distance from Grasmere to Manchester—but, in addition, Naylor had to ascend and descend about 35,000 feet, buffeted almost throughout by strong winds and often unable to see more than a few yards ahead. With better weather and moonlight it is likely that he would have been able to include Fairfield and Greatrigg Man which would have made a total of sixty-five peaks, and this, at the time of writing, remains the target for anybody who thinks he can do better. This, indeed, was the target that Alan Heaton had set himself, at the age of 45 in the summer of 1973, but bad weather caused him to abandon his attempt, after he had completed most of the round.

The present holder of the Lakeland 24 hours fell record which has been held down the years by many fine mountaineers, including Dr A. W. Wakefield who climbed on Everest and Eustace Thomas who climbed all the 4,000 metres peaks in the Alps, is a 37-year-old fell farmer who regularly runs round the Wasdale fells in the evening—just for the fun of it. I have never seen him out of breath, even at the end of a day's trotting over the fells, and he goes uphill quicker than most people can come down. At one time he used to suffer badly from cramp and other ailments—he once ran with an injured thigh after having been kicked by one of his cows—but he seems to be able to cope pretty well nowadays with salt tablets, glucose and fruit drinks. He is not remarkably fast on the descent but his staying power uphill and along undulating ground is quite phenomenal. Joss has accomplished many other tremendous feats in his homeland fells but has not confined himself to Lakeland on his long days out. The year following his record-breaking sixty-three peaks round he went to North Wales and set up a new record for the circuit of the fourteen 3,000-foot mountains in Snowdonia, taking only 4 hours 46 minutes to cover the course of 18 miles. He got temporarily crag-fast on Crib-Gogh, took cramp on Carnedd Dafydd and had some trouble with thick mist, but was able to knock nearly half an hour off the record that had been set up years earlier by Eric Beard, the likeable character who, you will remember, had improved on Alan Heaton's Lakeland 24 hours record in 1963.

Eric Beard—or 'Beardie', as we all knew him—was a spidery, little man with close-cropped hair and long thin legs who made mountains into mole hills. He ran up and down most of the highest mountains in England, Scotland, Ireland and Wales faster than anybody had done before, subsisting for the most part on honey or 'jam butties', became a legend in his lifetime, and died tragically at the age of 38. Had he been given just a few more years of life there is no knowing what he might have achieved. Almost certainly he would have put up endurance records in the mountains that might well have remained unequalled almost indefinitely and, as it is, some of his performances still stand unassailed, years after his untimely death.

'Beardie' seemed to have two passions in life—mountains and children—and nothing else seemed to matter. So long as he was in the mountains, climbing, walking, skiing or running, or helping or amusing the children, he was happy. He had no house and no car—just his tent, his mountain gear and his skis—but he never seemed to envy those with more possessions and more solid roots. Often he seemed to be without any proper sort of job but he would turn up in the Cairngorms, say, ready to turn his hand to anything so long as it took him into the mountains, while in the evenings he would give a turn at a ceilidh. I remember arriving at the Cairngorm car-park one wild, bitterly cold day many years ago to find the skiing slopes completely deserted, the runs sheeted in ice, the cloud down to ground level and the wind so strong it was difficult to stand up. Skiing was out of the question and I decided to try to drag myself up Cairngorm for the exercise when a little man almost hidden by an enormous rucksack, hung about with rope, crampons, pitons and ice-axe, arrived at the deserted Shieling. It was, of course, 'Beardie', the only other person about on the hill that day so far as I could see—off to meet a friend to climb an ice

Beinn Dearg Mhor

Sgurr Dearg and Inaccessible Pinnacle

The line of the Cuillin Ridge

gully in Coire an t-Sneachda. 'Grand day for the race, pal—the human race,' he piped in his high-pitched Yorkshire accent, as he disappeared into the mist. 'Keep yourself out of mischief.' On another day you might see him coming down the ski-run in Coire Cas on a tea-tray or on sawn-off skis, dressed in pyjamas and a fancy hat, or, perhaps, in the evening, when everybody was off the hill, trotting back up there, in the dusk, from Aviemore, in shorts and running shoes, just to keep his hand in. I had first met him when he arrived in the Lake District almost out of the blue, without apparent preparation, and proceeded to run round the fells for a day and a night—only stopping for an occasional 'jam buttie'—to add a further two peaks to Alan Heaton's fifty-four. Clearly, a new personality had arrived on the mountain scene, but his new Lakeland 24 hours fell record was only one of a long list of remarkable successes.

I have already referred to his record of the Welsh '3,000s' in the mid-sixties which stood until Joss Naylor improved upon it in 1973, and he had also done the Snowdon horseshoe in 1 hour 40 minutes. In 1963 Eric went to Ireland to tackle the Mountains of Mourne Walk—an annual event in which 200 or so walkers attempt to get round the 22 miles, with 10,000 feet of climbing, in less than 12 hours. He did it in 4 hours 26 minutes, and then looked round for something more difficult. He went to Scotland, did a midnight, moonlight traverse of the Cairngorm '4,000s' as a training session, and later, in a more serious attempt, completed the round in the remarkable time of 4 hours 41 minutes. From Glenmore Lodge he arrived on the summit of Braeriach in 96 minutes and reached Cairn Toul only 36 minutes later. For the steep descent to the Larig Ghru and the long climb to Ben Macdhui he required only 71 minutes, and 40 minutes later he was standing on the summit of Cairngorm. But perhaps his most remarkable feat in Scotland was his traverse of the Cuillin ridge in Skye, referred to in another chapter, which he did in 4 hours 9 minutes—thirty rock peaks, many of them requiring rock-climbing, in less time than most people take to get up and down Scafell Pike. He was accompanied to the first summit, Gars-bheinn, by a companion who then descended to Glen Brittle, planning to wait for Eric on the last summit, Sgurr nan Gillean, but the untiring little man from Leeds had got there first.

Eric did many other record walks and runs, often for charity. He trotted across the roof of Wales from north to south, and the length of Britain from John o' Groats to Land's End. Many people have climbed Ben Nevis, Scafell Pike and Snowdon, the three highest mountains in Scotland, England and Wales, within 24 hours—with a driver to take them along the intervening distances by car—but Eric, scorning the use of transport, did the whole distance on foot. But in November 1969, on his way to yet another 24 hours run, in aid of the Save the Children Fund, Eric was killed in a road accident. He was only 38 years of age, and hundreds of people in the mountain world knew that a remarkable man and most lovable personality had passed from their midst.

Mountain running has thrown up many interesting personalities over the years for, clearly, men who like to run uphill as well as down, and often at night, just for the fun of it, and are prepared to carry on almost until they drop, are hardly ordinary, run-of-the-mill people. They come in all shapes and sizes—although none are fat—from all walks of life, and from most age groups. One of the most remarkable of them is a manufacturer of tripe and cow heel—when he can spare the time away from the mountains—who is still covering enormous distances at the trot at the age of 62. Stanley Bradshaw of Padiham near Burnley is a short, bald-headed man with a merry face, who has run up and down hundreds of mountains throughout Britain and done many amazingly long walks stretching across several counties. He was the second man to cover the Bob Graham round of forty-two Lakeland peaks within 24 hours—Alan Heaton, as already stated, having been the first—and managed to knock a few minutes off Graham's time. Graham had been 43 years of age when he did his round in 1932 but Bradshaw was 48 when he repeated it, and, to date, is the oldest man to have done so, and, I think, the oldest man to have attempted it. But Stan Bradshaw has become well accustomed, during the past twenty years or so, to being the oldest man taking part in all sorts of fell races and extremely long walks, and he seems to thrive on it.

The flat-topped bulk of Ingleborough in Yorkshire was the first mountain that Stan ever climbed but he has long lost count of the total of his subsequent ascents. The first Three Peaks race, over the summits of Ingleborough, Whernside and Pen-y-Ghent, was staged in 1954 and Stan finished second to F. C. Bagley, out of only eight competitors. Nowadays, such is the interest in the event that competitors have to be restricted to 300, for safety reasons. Of the twenty Three Peaks races that had been held up to 1973, Stan had competed nineteen times and finished the course on eighteen occasions. He estimates that, including walking and training, he must have been round the Three Peaks more than seventy times, which means that he probably knows these lonely fells better than anybody else. Some years ago when I was proposing to go round myself but was not certain of the exact route I wrote to Stan asking if he could provide the necessary information. He wrote back, enclosing a rough sketch map he had done for me that included such helpful details as 'bog', 'drainage ditch', 'gap in wall' and 'dead sheep in beck', which at least suggested that his information was up-to-date. The walk, if you are not racing, makes a long day for most people—elsewhere in the book I refer to my own humble circumnavigations—but the fell runners' record in 1973 was an incredible 2 hours 31 minutes 58 seconds by Geoff Norman of Altrincham.

The Rucksack Club, of which Stan Bradshaw is a member, are pioneers of long-distance walks over moors and mountains, one of these being the Tan Hill Walk linking the two highest pubs in England—the Tan Hill in north Yorkshire and the Cat and the Fiddle in Cheshire. The distance is about 120 miles with a total ascent and descent of nearly 20,000 feet and it is clearly one of the most formidable walks in England. Six or seven years ago Stan, assuming, incorrectly, 'that my running days would soon be only a memory', decided, with two friends, Dennis Weir and John Richardson, to tackle it in winter and left a family party on the evening of Boxing Day to reach the start of the walk. They left Tan Hill in driving sleet, encountered snow, mist, high winds and driving rain, but kept on over the backbone of England, over the fells and across the moors for two days and two nights, to complete the walk, in hail, thunder and lightning in 51 hours 49 minutes. Stan remembers standing in a horse trough on one occasion to cool off his burning feet and towards the end the three of them were dozing off as they walked, waking again when they bumped into each other.

There are twelve mountain summits in Britain over 4,000 feet high, all of them in Scotland. Nine of them are in the Cairngorms and three are in the Ben Nevis area and they were first all climbed in one expedition about fifty years ago. This was a splendid achievement but in the middle of the 1950s the hard men of the Rucksack

Club spotted an obvious weakness in the expedition in that a car had been used to convey the walkers from the Ben Nevis group to the Cairngorms which lie about sixty miles apart. They therefore resolved to cut out the motoring and walk the whole way, the feat finally being achieved at Whitsuntide 1954. The round from Fort William to Coylum Bridge near Aviemore worked out at 98 miles, the total height ascended to something over 13,000 feet and the first complete walk took about 52 hours. Stan Bradshaw, of course, had to have a shot at this and completed the round of the 'Scottish Fours', as the walk is loosely described, in 1967 at the age of 55. He and his companion left Fort William for the ascent of Ben Nevis at 8.30 p.m. on the Friday evening and arrived at Coylum Bridge, with the twelve summits and about 100 miles of walking behind them, at 8.30 the following Monday morning. They were disappointed that they had taken 60 hours on the walk across the highest land in Scotland, but they had lost at least eight hours through being benighted by blizzards on both Ben Nevis and Ben Macdhui.

And the following year Stan did an even more remarkable walk—the traverse of all the summits in the Lake District over 2,500 feet in one continuous round. Three of them did the whole walk, with two supporters for part of the way, and they went over no fewer than seventy-seven summits which meant a walk of 105 miles with 43,065 feet of ascent—one and a half Everests. They started from the Duddon early on the Saturday morning, first going over the Coniston fells, and they finished at Low Hartsop in Patterdale at five o'clock on the Tuesday morning. During the three days and three nights they had been over all the high land in the Lake District, having difficulty in finding some of the summits because of thick cloud. The three were very tired towards the end of the walk, so much so that in the High Street area they had the sensation of walking through trees and noticed that the stones in cairns were beginning to spin. It is interesting to note that the late Eustace Thomas who held the Lakeland 24 hours fell record for many years until it was broken by Bob Graham in 1932 went round the 'Lakes 2,500s' about fifty years ago. He spent the nights in inns and took five days to complete a roughly similar course.

This, of course, is one of the serious problems in these very long walks—the difficulty of carrying on without any sleep. Stan has trained himself to cope with the situation but he needed all his resolution on a tremendous walk during the Easter of 1968 when he linked the highest points of England's six northern counties in one long expedition. The walk covered 145 miles and was completed in 73 hours—believed to be the longest continuous mountain walk ever carried out in British hills. Stan, who was 55 years of age at the time, described it afterwards as 'an enjoyable holiday walk'. This is one man's way of spending his holidays; his next holiday was the 'Lakes 2,500s'. Not much time for relaxing. The six counties walk was planned in secret for, as in rock climbing, new ventures are liable to be forestalled by competitors if news leaks out. Four of them started on the marathon but two had to drop out and only Stan and Brian Ripley, 24 years old, completed the walk. Later the same year Ripley was killed during a Manchester expedition to the Karakorum—a tragic ending to a short but brilliant mountain career.

The county tops in the order of ascent were: The Cheviot, 2,676 feet (Northumberland); Burnhope Seat, 2,452 feet (Durham); Mickle Fell, 2,591 feet (Yorkshire); Helvellyn, 3,118 feet (Westmorland); Scafell Pike, 3,210 feet (Cumberland); and Coniston Old Man, 2,633 feet (Lancashire). (These were the heights of these mountains in 1968 but, since then, the Ordnance Survey have knocked off a few feet, here and there!) The party started at Langley Fold, Northumberland at 1.30 a.m. on Good Friday morning and Stan and Brian reached the Walna Scar track above Coniston early on the Tuesday morning. This meant nearly four nights without sleep and Stan said afterwards that he thought that three nights was getting towards the maximum. On the fourth night out both men were so tired they were delirious and having hallucinations—according to their support man who provided meals at pre-determined points. As they were coming down Moasdale on their way from Scafell Pike to Coniston Old Man Stan thought he could see concrete houses, although he knows well that the dale is without habitation, and once he tried to walk round a small puddle, thinking it was a fair-sized tarn. And Stan agreed afterwards that although he knew Coniston Old Man like the back of his hand he had been so tired at the end that the mountain seemed completely strange to him.

Brian Ripley and his brother Allan had carried out an even more remarkable walk the previous year—the traverse of no fewer than 230 Scottish Munros* in one go—but although this was an almost

* A 'Munro' is a separate Scottish mountain over 3,000 feet in height.

incredible performance it could hardly be classed as a continuous mountain walk for the two sometimes stayed in huts, bothies and shooting lodges along the way. Nevertheless it was probably the longest and most gruelling mountain expedition ever achieved in this country and failed, by only forty-seven peaks, in its original objective of ticking off all the Munros in one walk. The walk lasted for thirteen weeks and finished at Bridge of Balgie in November after the two had covered 1,325 miles and climbed up and down something like 337,850 feet. By that time their ankles were swollen and sore, they were running into bad weather and they were falling behind schedule. They had started on 13 August from a camp by the shore of Loch Hope, and their first Munro was the most northerly one, Ben Hope. In a zigzag course they moved southwards through Scotland, ticking off all the Munros in turn, and had intended to finish on the most southerly Munro, Ben Lomond, but the conditions proved too much for them. Three of them had started out but David Summerfield was forced to abandon the walk after six weeks. Their long round included the traverse of the Cuillin ridge in Skye where they encountered rain and mist but completed the ridge in 15 hours. Throughout the long walk they carried heavy packs and camped on many occasions. Mount Keen, the most easterly Munro, was reached on 12 October and thereafter they had appalling weather for much of the time. On Beinn Dorain above Rannoch Moor the wind was so strong that they had to crawl on all fours at times, and one morning in Glen Affric their tent collapsed over them during breakfast. But they went up Ben Nevis in 90 minutes and did most of the Mamores in one day, demonstrating their superb fitness. This was a remarkable marathon that, but for bad weather, would have made mountaineering history.

Perhaps the most famous long-distance walkers' route in England is the Pennine Way—270 miles of mountain and moorland from Edale in Derbyshire to Kirk Yetholm just over the Scottish border. Most people take about a fortnight to complete the walk, staying at youth hostels, cottages and inns along the way, although several have done it in a shorter time. Alan Heaton, the first man to break Bob Graham's Lakeland 24 hours record, and Michael Meath from Barnoldswick, did the walk in June 1972 in 4 days, 5 hours and 10 minutes which, at the time of writing, stands as the record so far as those who must get their walks over as quickly as possible are concerned.* They left Edale at one o'clock on a Friday afternoon and walked to the Widdop road near Hebden Bridge, a distance of 47 miles, in 9 hours 15 minutes. Thinking this was enough for half a day they then went home to bed but were back at Widdop road bright and early the next morning prepared for a really long day. For nearly 15½ hours they walked and trotted along the backbone of England until they reached Thwaite and then camped for the night at Keld, not far away, having added another 70 miles. This was to be their longest day, so far as distance was concerned, but on the third day they covered 61½ miles to Garrigill near Alston in 15 hours 20 minutes and, on the day after that, a further 50½ miles to Bellingham in 15½ hours. For three days, therefore, they had been walking for more than 15 hours a day and covering an average of 60 miles daily, although, naturally, the distances were decreasing. On the last day, therefore, they took it fairly easily, covering the remaining 41 miles in just over 12 hours and finishing on the village green outside the inn at Kirk Yetholm at the run just after six o'clock in the evening. Remarkably, they didn't go into the pub for a pint but drank tea on the green, quietly content, no doubt, that a long weekend was over and that one more record could go into the books. Alan, who was 44 years old at the time, finished with two small blisters but otherwise seemed no more distressed than the average tourist who has just walked down to Seathwaite from Scafell Pike. Michael, at 25 the youngest person to have completed the walk in anything approaching this remarkable time, escaped without blisters but confessed to being a little leg-weary. Both men had breakfasted and dined heartily each day and slept well, but on the walk itself largely kept going on liquids and glucose. Three friends accompanied them along parts of the route and the one who did the longest distances was Stan Bradshaw who, at 60 years of age, thought nothing of carrying their packs. It was Alan's second attempt to set up a record for the Pennine Way. The previous year he had tried to do it solo but had had to abandon his attempt because of tendon trouble after covering 186 miles.

So many long-distance mountain races and marathon walks are being organized nowadays that no more than a brief summary of some of them is possible here. There is, for instance, the Lyke Wake Walk of 40 miles across the North Yorkshire Moors which

* In June, 1974, Joss Naylor did the Pennine Way in 3 days 4 hours, 46 minutes—by not sleeping.

has its own mournful Lyke Wake Dirge, possibly the oldest dialect verse in the country. I remember, during a traverse of the Lakeland '3,000s' a few years ago, that my companion kept chanting this dirge, with its dreadful premonitions of death and disaster, as we were crawling up Skiddaw in darkness, mist and drizzle. At the time it seemed depressingly doleful but appropriate. The Lyke Wake Walk was first done as an expedition in 1955 in 13 hours walking time, but has since become a national institution with, it is reported, more than 45,000 crossings by 1972. There is now a Lyke Wake Club with Bill Cowley, the originator, as Chief Dirger, and many humorous connotations, and the record, for those who want to take it at the run—which was perhaps not the original intention—stood at less than 5 hours in 1973. Another annual event is the Fellsman Hike of about 55 miles over thirteen Yorkshire mountains which was first held in 1962, after a projected inauguration the previous year had been thwarted by deep snow. Although 57 competitors started on the first event only 15 finished, but of the nearly 400 starters in 1972 a total of 236 got round the course. So great is the interest in this event nowadays that more than 1,000 people apply to take part each year but only 400 are accepted. The 1972 winner took less than 16 hours to complete the course and the event has been won on six occasions by Alan Heaton, the former holder of the Lakeland 24 hours fell record, while the ubiquitous Stan Bradshaw has completed the course seven times.

In the Lake District there are several mountain races and trials including circuits of both the Ennerdale and Wasdale hills in which, naturally, Joss Naylor, who lives at the foot of these fells, has been especially prominent. Joss has also won the Vaux Lake District Mountain Trial, which is run over a different route each year, more often than anybody else. In this event competitors start at intervals and link up a series of check points, indicated to them at the start by map references, returning to the start after a run of about 20 miles over some of the most difficult mountain country the course-planners can find. In some years the trial has been based at Wasdale Head and on one of these occasions, not long after the start of his mountain running career, Joss Naylor entered and come in an easy first. It was discovered, however, that he had failed to report at one of the check points which happened to be the summit of Seatallan, just over 2 miles away from where he farms, and he had to be disqualified. He said later that he did not know Seatallan,

The Martindale Fells

Summit ridge of Blencathra

High Street range from Sheffield Pike

Pen-y-Ghent

Whernside

Ingleborough

which I find difficult to believe—somebody said his sheep didn't go that far—but whether or not he was pulling our legs he certainly knows it now. Another Lake District event is the walk over the 3,000 feet tops which I write about elsewhere in this book. This is supposed to be a walk, as distinct from a race, but naturally some runners use the occasion to test themselves out and, naturally again, Joss Naylor has done the round faster than anybody else—in an incredible 8 hours 20 minutes. Most people would be very proud to do the feat—Skiddaw, the Scafells and Helvellyn, starting and finishing at Keswick—in twice this time, and some of those who take part in the annual walk promoted by the Ramblers Association take 20 hours or more. When Naylor went round he was so much faster than anybody had expected that the checkers had not arrived on the top of Helvellyn by the time he reached the summit and he had to leave a scribbled note to show that he had gone through.

This far-from-complete record of long-distance running in the fells, in which I have mentioned a few of the outstanding performances but missed out many more names than I have included, would be even more incomplete if I failed to mention a very exclusive club—one of the most exclusive in the country—that has emerged out of all these years of effort and determination. This is the Bob Graham 24 Hours Club—the memorial, if you like, to the Borrowdale guest-house proprietor who on 13 June 1932, at the age of 43, set off at the run from Keswick market place at one o'clock in the morning and proceeded to trot up and down half the mountains in the Lake District at one go. He arrived back in Keswick in 21 minutes under the 24 hours after the longest mountain 'walk' in history at that time and was up at six o'clock the same morning to cook breakfast for the companions who had accompanied him along the different sections of the route.

All you have to do to join the Bob Graham Club is to run up and down the same forty-two mountains that he did, within 24 hours. The long day comes to about 80 miles, with a total height of rather more than the height of Everest, and this particular round has now come to be regarded as the sort of lodestar of the long-distance mountain runner. As I write in the autumn of 1973 only sixteen people have completed the round and two of them—Bob Graham himself and Eric Beard—are dead. The remaining fourteen are full members of the Club and each has a certificate to prove it, the only reward for a great deal of energy and determination. It is not awarded for the ascent of *any* forty-two Lake District mountains within the day for it would easily be possible to devise a round embracing forty-two summits that did not involve anything like the effort required in Graham's big walk. The certificate, therefore, goes to anybody who completes the Graham round within 24 hours, starting and finishing at the Moot Hall, Keswick, near the market place, but going either clockwise or counter-clockwise round the forty-two tops—Graham went clockwise. It may also be awarded to people who complete a circuit of the fells, based on the Graham round, within 24 hours, but including other peaks as well, which, at the discretion of the committee 'constitutes a more meritorious achievement, either by reason of extra peaks climbed, height ascended, or time taken'. This rule enables the Club to invite to membership those supermen who, in recent years, have been up and down many more peaks than Graham during the day but may have missed out one or two of the tops covered on the 1932 'walk'. The basic requirement, however, remains the Graham round which seems a sufficiently high standard for any mountain runner.

Graham first went up Skiddaw, Great Calva and Blencathra and then along the Dodds, the Helvellyn range and Fairfield. He then crossed Dunmail Raise and did all the Langdale tops followed by Bowfell and the Scafells before descending to Wasdale Head. Yewbarrow and the whole of the Red Pike-Pillar range came next, followed by Kirk Fell and the Gables and the Buttermere fells. At midnight Graham was near Newlands Hause and seven miles from home but he ran it all the way in 39 minutes, finishing under the clock in the market place with 21 minutes to spare. I remember I had the pleasure of introducing the Heaton brothers to Bob Graham on the top of Honister Pass during Alan's record run in 1960. Mr Graham, then a rather portly 71, briefly recalled his run of twenty-eight years earlier and wished them every success. In the 1950s Graham told me he was very surprised that his record was then still standing, adding: 'Anybody should be able to get round in the day—provided he's fit enough,' which seemed to me something of an over-simplification. Not many people are able to achieve this sort of supreme fitness. Graham reckoned that when he went round in 1932 he rested on the uphill stretches, which may seem to some people an extraordinary statement, but I can understand what he meant. When you are running downhill your feet, knees, thighs and arms are working hard all the time and your body is being badly shaken up. It must come almost as a relief—provided you have the necessary fitness—to change from this quick, juddering descent to a much slower, rhythmical ascent, although those of us who puff and blow going uphill may not always appreciate this.

The oldest of the fourteen Club members is, of course, the ever-youthful Stan Bradshaw who got round in 1960 when he was a mere 48 years of age. The fastest time for the round up to 1973 was 20 hours 38 minutes set up by W. B. Millen and W. E. Smith in August of that year. The youngest runner to complete the round was then Michael Meath who went round in 1971 when only 24 years of age. A few people have completed the Graham round but taken a little more than 24 hours but, such is the rigour of the game, these are denied full membership. The man who started the Bob Graham Club is Mr Fred Rogerson of Windermere who has been involved, as organizer, in all the attempts since 1960.

Long-distance mountain running is a growing sport attracting an increasing number of people who value physical fitness and see the hills as a worthwhile challenge. At one time a handful of diehards deplored the turning of the mountains into race tracks, but a few runners or long-distance walkers in any one event should not embarrass the most aesthetically-minded consciences. The runners may not be seeing much of the scenery but they're not harming it, either, and the events are carefully organized so as to avoid trespass or damage to land or property. Lakeland has a tradition of professional fell-running going back as far as the 1850s or earlier—local farmers and shepherds racing one another up and down the nearest fell for small money prizes. The earliest Grasmere Sports records show that a J. Fleming won the guides race, as the event is named, in 1852 but it is likely that fell-racing in something like its present form did not begin at these sports until 1868 when G. Birkett ran up and down Silver Howe in 22 minutes and picked up £3 for his trouble. Nowadays, the race is run up and down Butter Crags, the record of 13 minutes 5 seconds having been set up in 1965 by W. Teasdale, a Caldbeck shepherd, at the age of 40. Teasdale is the most remarkable professional fell-runner of modern times, perhaps of all time, having won the Grasmere event eleven times and been honoured by the Queen with the award of the M.B.E. But these professional fell races, held in many parts of the Lake District and the north of England, are of no more than passing interest here where I am mainly concerned with long days in the hills. Even some of the amateur fell races held over much longer courses are still only regarded as short distance events—by long-distance runners although not, perhaps, by fell walkers. It is 10 miles from Fitz Park, Keswick to the top of Skiddaw and back but David Cannon has done the distance in 2½ minutes over the hour (1973). The same runner has also run round the eight tops of the Fairfield horseshoe in 1 hour 8½ minutes (1972)—an expedition to which some fell walkers, savouring the views, might devote most of a day, while walkers wasting no time in stops might need half a day to get round. Other Lake District 'horseshoe' races include the circuits of the Ennerdale, Wasdale and Langdale fells and the multiplication of these events is only restricted by the number of weekends in the sporting-calendar. More ambitious, perhaps, are the two-day 'marathons' in which competitors, carrying all their equipment, camp out for one night.

There are, of course, no monetary awards for these amateur events, although successful competitors generally receive handsome gifts in kind, mostly mountain wear and equipment. But the people who complete the Bob Graham round of forty-two Lakeland peaks in the day or who do the Scottish 'four thousands' in one continuous walk or who struggle on for days and nights on the big walks of the Rucksack Club get nothing tangible for their pains—except for the certificate given to newly-qualified members of the Bob Graham Club. Their rewards are just the personal satisfaction that they have survived particularly demanding tests of physical endurance, but many mountain folk will agree that this is a very worthwhile prize. Those who complete the rather dubious achievement of standing on the tops of Ben Nevis, Scafell Pike and Snowdon within the day—dubious because it is a test of transport and driver as much as of the mountaineer—sometimes get their names in the papers, although I don't remember any fuss being made when Eric Beard quietly shamed them all by walking all the way. Two incidents have long made me suspicious of this Ben Nevis – Scafell Pike – Snowdon gimmick. The first was when I was once accosted on Styhead by three youths who told me they were making a reconnaissance before doing the round a day or two later. They then left me and started walking up Great Gable and I had to shout back and tell them they were on the wrong mountain. When they came down they admitted they didn't know where Scafell Pike lay and asked me to show them the way. The second incident was when I was attending a climbing club meet at Brackenclose, Wasdale. Two of us were standing near the hut when we saw a helicopter flying towards us over Wastwater. The machine landed not far away and two or three men, oddly dressed for the mountains, scrambled out and asked us the way to Scafell Pike. When we indicated the way up Brown Tongue they informed us they were attempting the 'three peaks record' and promptly hurried away at a speed I'm sure they did not maintain to the summit. My companion at the time was the late Bentley Beetham, the well-known climbing pioneer who had been on one of the early Everest expeditions, and I wish I could remember his typical caustic comments.

There seems little in these achievements of three mountains in a day separated by a great deal of motoring—generally with somebody else at the wheel—to compare with Joss Naylor's sixty-three mountains within 24 hours in bad weather and Stanley Bradshaw's seventy-seven Lakeland summits in three days and nights of walking or his 145 miles walk over the tops of the six northern counties. Not to mention Heaton and Meath's Pennine Way epic in something over four days. All these long-distance record-breakers, runners and walkers, are people who have tested out their stamina to its farthest limits, and it may not be a bad thing to know just how far your own determination and body will take you. Few of us test ourselves to the limit—it requires great dedication, determination, and time and it always hurts—and at least these record-breakers know themselves pretty well. And so in these days when sporting personalities make a great deal of money in their public performances, these quiet men of the mountains, whose achievements are no less praiseworthy but who do it all for 'fun', deserve our respect and admiration.

THE LONELY RAVINE

Most regular visitors to the fells know the pools and waterfalls of the Esk, the Duddon and, perhaps, the Langstrath Beck, but not so many are familiar with the ravines of Nether Beck which are among the finest in the district. Nether Beck slides unobtrusively into Wastwater, about halfway along its northern shore, but its placid emergence round the corner through the trees gives no suggestion of its real character. Its two main feeders are a spring high up in the Pillar range and the lonely pool of Scoat Tarn, and its southwards course to the deepest lake in England is in the form of a gigantic S, three miles long. The lower half of the beck is the most interesting for here it has carved great ravines through the rock—in places a hundred feet deep. Hanging over the ravines the rowans have formed dark tunnels and down the gorge are waterfalls crashing between contorted pillars of rock and dark pools that rarely see the sun. From the boggy track winding up the valley little is seen or heard of this wonder and tumult, but an airy sheep-trod along the wall of the ravine provides viewpoints for the slightly more adventurous explorer. Scoat Tarn lies nearly 2,000 feet above sea-level in a rock basin not far below the splendid ridge of Red Pike and by its boulder-strewn shores you can laze away a summer afternoon and probably never see anything move except sheep and clouds. South-east across the trough of Wasdale the highest land in England is notched across the sky but the processions over Scafell Pike are too far away to be seen and few people seek out the lonely western fells around Seatallan.

7

The Cuillin Ridge

A History and a Traverse

The Black Cuillin, a curving range of jagged rock peaks hidden away in the south-east corner of Skye, are the most spectacular mountains in the British Isles. Almost bare of vegetation they rise in steep screes and grey-black crags to a shattered ridge of towers, pinnacles and airy ledges—at one end high above the sea; elsewhere, overlooking lonely corries and deserted glens. The summits of almost all other mountains in Britain may be reached by simple, rough walking, but only a few of the rock peaks of the Black Cuillin are accessible to the ordinary walker, and then only by scrambling and the use of the hands, while many of the tops are only attainable by rock-climbing. These were the last mountains in Britain to be climbed—half of them only within the last 100 years—and the last one of all, Sgurr Coir' an Lochain, was only climbed for the first time in 1896.

There are many theories about the derivation of the name Cuillin, and many different spellings. The probability is that it comes from Old Norse and was first coined by the Vikings who were in the area about one thousand years ago. One rather fanciful theory is that the name is derived from a Gaelic word meaning 'holly' and it is true that the skyline of the mountains as seen from the sea has something of the shape of a holly-leaf, but this suggested variation is largely discounted nowadays. The Cuillin is a term which loosely embraces all the main mountains in the waist of Skye, but there are really two Cuillins—the Red Cuillin and the Black Cuillin. The first-named group of hills, of reddish granite, are steep but rounded and therefore of little interest to the mountaineer;

the second group are largely of gabbro—a black, extremely rough, almost prickly rock that offers the best possible hand and footholds for the climber. This rock is so sound and so wrinkled with knobs and excrescences that more or less vertical places can often be climbed with comparative ease, and crags that would look formidable on the mainland peaks can, in the Black Cuillin, be confidently tackled. Gabbro, although so safe, is very demanding on the fingers, and after a day's climbing—or even scrambling—in the Cuillin the hands are often pricked with blood. Less safe for climbing is the basalt which appears as weathered dykes or ridges in the gabbro and is often loose, smooth, and slippery, especially when wet. It has been said that the only other place in Britain where gabbro may be found is in the adjoining island of Rhum, but in fact there are small gabbro crags on Carrock Fell in northern Lakeland.

The horseshoe ridge of the Black Cuillin includes twenty peaks, most of them around 3,000 feet high, and the ridge never drops below 2,500 feet. Some of the peaks have several pointed summits—Sgurr a' Mhadaidh, for instance, has four—and if you count all the pinnacles and tops along the ridge there are thirty-two to be climbed. The ridge is about 8 miles long and to reach it and return to the glen requires a further 8 miles of walking. Much of the ridge involves scrambling and easy climbing but there are four sections of quite difficult rock-climbing, normally requiring the use of the rope. You cannot run along the ridge of the Black Cuillin as you can along the Lakeland ridges, for the hands are needed for much of the way and in mist the way is difficult to find. Subsidiary ridges leave the main ridge at puzzling angles in several places, and compasses, on this rock, are unreliable. And a further difficulty, on such a dry, rocky ridge-pole on a hot day, is that there is not one drop of water along the whole of its length, unless you can find rainwater in crevices in the rocks. There is no other ridge of rock mountains anything like this in the British Isles—nothing so long, with so much rock and so many peaks; nothing so dramatic or so rewarding. For the traverse of the main ridge of the Black Cuillin is the finest mountaineering expedition in this country—not, of course, the most difficult, but certainly the most varied and exhilarating.

But for many years the traverse within one day was considered an impossibility. The early climbers had often taken long days just to explore short sections of the ridge, and to complete the whole length, up and down every peak from Gars-bheinn in the south to

The Cuillin Ridge

On the Cuillin Ridge

Coire a' Ghrunnda and Sgurr Alasdair

Sgurr nan Gillean in the north, was thought to be quite beyond the powers of even exceptional mountaineers. If the traverse was started from Glen Brittle, the nearest base to the southern end of the ridge, it would first involve an extremely rough walk of 3 or 4 miles round the coast and across the foot of the corries, and then the ascent of Gars-bheinn—nearly 3,000 feet of back-breaking toil up steep, unstable screes. The contenders would then be at the start of the ridge with thirty summits and pinnacles ahead of them before they reached Sgurr nan Gillean, the last peak, and the long, rough descent to the Sligachan Inn. After Gars-bheinn ('the echoing mountain') would come rough scrambling over Sgurr a' Choire Bhig and then a long descent and a 500-feet climb to Sgurr nan Eag ('the notched peak'), followed by scrambling over Caisteal a' Gharbh-choire ('the castle of the rough corrie') and a climb up the rough slabs of Sgurr Dubh na Da Bheinn ('the black peak of the two hills'). At this point it is easy in mist to make the mistake of continuing over the Dubhs towards Coruisk, but the correct course is to swing north-west down to the Bealach Coir an Lochain, from which there would be an escape for the weary into the corrie and thence back to Glen Brittle. But to continue the ridge it would be necessary to carry on up to the Thearlaich-Dubh gap—the first serious difficulty.

This gap, which was first crossed in 1891, involves the descent of a vertical wall 25 feet high, and the ascent, from the other side of the narrow gap, of an 80 feet high wall of slabs and chimneys which is not quite so steep. It is difficult to escape from the gap if the ascent of either side proves too demanding and an early instruction to climbers in the first guide-book was to be careful not to have all members of the party in the gap at the same time—in case they might have to remain there for ever! After the gap has been crossed there is the ascent to the summit of Sgurr Thearlaich ('the peak of Charles' named after Charles Pilkington who first climbed it), although most people doing the ridge nowadays first cross to the summit of Sgurr Alasdair, the highest summit of the Cuillin named after Sheriff Alexander Nicolson but not, strictly speaking, on the ridge itself, and then descend and ascend to the top of Sgurr Thearlaich. The descent of steep slabs, which can be very tricky when wet, is then made to the rocky col below the vertical prow of Sgurr Mhic Coinnich ('Mackenzie's peak') which has the second rock-climbing problem on the traverse. This is King's Chimney, a steep climb on good holds and then a traverse below an overhang on to easier ground and the summit, although there is an easier alternative round the face to the left known as Collie's Ledge.

At this point, thought the early climbers, they would be less than halfway along the ridge, with many problems still ahead of them. First, there would be the descent to the Bealach Coire Lagan and then a tiring ascent of about 500 feet up sliding screes over the peak of An Stac to the Inaccessible Pinnacle—a huge finger of rock sticking up above the summit of Sgurr Dearg ('the red peak'). This would have to be traversed by an exposed but easy route up one side and then descended by the slightly overhanging prow of the pinnacle, probably on a doubled rope. Then would follow, in succession, the traverse of the many rocky summits of Sgurr na Banachdich ('the milkmaid's peak'), Sgurr Thormaid ('Norman's peak' named after Professor Collie, who did much of the early pioneering in Skye and died there during the last war), Sgurr a' Ghreadaidh ('the peak of the mighty winds') and Sgurr a' Mhadaidh ('the fox's peak') which, on their own, can often make a normal day's expedition. But the three peaks of Bidean Druim nan Ramh ('the peak of the ridge of oars') would next have to be tackled—presenting one of the more difficult route-finding problems of the whole ridge—and then the long plod to Bruach na Frithe ('the brae of the forest'), one of the most tiring sections. And ahead of Bruach na Frithe would be the fearsome obstacle of the Bhasteir Tooth—a great wall of vertical rock that would have to be climbed to its crest, followed by the ascent of 'The Executioner' (Am Basteir) itself, with its last awkward pitch just below the summit. The end would now be in sight, but there would still be the climb up the rocky west ridge of Sgurr nan Gillean ('the peak of the young men'), past the gendarme known as 'The Policeman', before reaching the final summit, and the long rough walk down the glen to Sligachan.

This was the measure of the Cuillin ridge and there were mountaineers eighty years ago who thought that its traverse would take three days. But early this century George Abraham, the Keswick climber who died in his nineties in 1965, thought that the traverse of the ridge in a day might be possible some day by a climber with the necessary endurance and technique, although he doubted whether such a superman could be found. But a few years later, in June 1911, two such men appeared on the scene, and although considerable sections of the ridge were unknown to them they succeeded in making the complete traverse for the first time, reaching Sligachan nearly 17 hours after they left Glen Brittle and taking 12 hours 18 minutes along the ridge. 'The bogey has now been laid for ever,' wrote Ashley Abraham, George's brother, shortly afterwards, adding that the feat had been 'one of the most remarkable feats of endurance and mountaineering and climbing skill ever accomplished in our home mountains.'

The two climbers were L. G. Shadbolt and A. G. MacLaren, members of the Scottish Mountaineering Club who had been visiting Skye for about five years. They left Glen Brittle at 3.35 a.m., reached the top of the first peak, Gars-bheinn in 2½ hours, and the end of the ridge at 6.25 p.m., arriving at Sligachan Inn 3 hours later. Apparently the two did not bother to lay caches of food and water along the ridge, carried their own ropes and supplies, and eschewed the aid of pacers or parties with provisions, and this was to be the pattern of most of the many successful attempts that were to follow. Shadbolt and MacLaren found themselves 2½ hours ahead of their schedule when they reached the summit of Sgurr Dearg, although the round of Coire Lagan—an unfamiliar section of the ridge to them—had taken longer than planned. Altogether they spent about 2½ hours in resting at various points along the ridge and towards the end of the walk were suffering from thirst. To get water they had to leave the ridge shortly after Bruach na Frithe and scramble down into Sgurr a' Fionn Choire where there is a tiny pool among the rocks. But they finished quite fresh and must have been very happy men as they sat down for their celebration drink in the Sligachan Inn.

The feat attracted a great deal of attention in the mountaineering world but, strangely enough, it was nine years before the traverse was repeated. Shadbolt and MacLaren had proved that the traverse of the ridge in one day was a feasible venture for climbers possessing the necessary stamina and skill, but there are no records of anyone else even attempting the feat until it was eventually carried out in 1920 by T. H. Somervell, the Kendal surgeon-mountaineer who was later to reach nearly 28,000 feet on Everest and is now living in retirement in Ambleside. Somervell set off with a companion but did most of the ridge on his own and felt so fresh on Sgurr nan Gillean that he carried on to Sgurr na h-Uamha which he thought should be regarded as the real end of the traverse. He took something over 14 hours for the complete round—less than 11 hours on the ridge itself—and said afterwards that with a water-bottle and a pound of raisins he could have knocked an hour off his time. It was, he thought, the finest expedition outside the Alps.

After that the traverse of the main ridge became increasingly popular. The first woman to accomplish the feat (Dr M. M. Barker who lived at one time at Caldbeck in Cumberland) did so in 1926, and two years later came the first traverse by an all-women's party. Many people failed on the ridge, through exhaustion or thirst, but more and more people successfully completed the traverse—first, perhaps one or two parties in a season and then several until, by the outbreak of war, at least thirty people had achieved the feat. In 1932 Peter Bicknell put up the then record time of just under 12 hours, including 8 hours spent on the ridge, while a few people were able to make second traverses, and one or two to make the crossing several times. The ridge has been traversed at night and people have camped on top, taking it comfortably and enjoying the views without hurrying. Several times the ridge has been traversed from north to south, which makes it slightly harder, while the aim has often been to start and finish at Glen Brittle, making it a longer round, or at Loch Coruisk, which is much shorter. Perhaps the finest expedition of all was that of 1965 when the ridge was done in winter, with the whole traverse plastered in snow and ice, a very strong four-man party led by the late Dr Tom Patey and the Everest climber, Hamish McInnes, taking two days to complete the crossing. Meanwhile, faster and faster times were set up, the time for the ridge being eventually cut down to 6 or 7 hours. I am not sure how the 'record' stands at present, but I do know that the remarkable Eric Beard, a most lovable and entertaining personality who was killed a few years ago in a car accident, completed the traverse in the 1960s in the fantastic ridge time of 4 hours 9 minutes. This must have meant running or trotting most of the way, although there is hardly a level ten yards along the whole ridge, and scampering up and down rock-climbs at the sort of speed that, for most people, would be suicidal. But Eric, who captured most of the mountain endurance records in Britain in his quite amazing career, made his own rules as he went along. One of the much-publicized but highly controversial feats of mountain record-breakers is to go up and down Ben Nevis, Snowdon, and Scafell Pike—the highest mountains in Scotland, Wales and England—in a day, which is largely a test of the motorist and his car. Eric did the same round, taking rather longer—but he walked all the way.

The fine rocky peaks of Blaven and Clach Glas are of the same geological structure as the mountains along the main ridge, but are separated from it by the lonely reaches of Glen Sligachan. Some of the early ridge climbers, notably Howard Somervell, wondered whether it might be possible, some day, for exceptional people to complete the round of the gabbro peaks within 24 hours by including Blaven and Clach Glas. It would obviously be an exceptional challenge, with a descent almost to sea-level after the traverse of the ridge, the long walk down and across the glen and then the ascent of two more mountains, but the feat was accomplished in 1939 by I. C. Charleson and W. E. Forde with a total ridge time of 20 hours. They laid caches of food beforehand, used three tents—one in Harta Corrie between the main ridge and Blaven—and also carried an alarm-clock. A month later J. K. Cooke, F. B. Dutton-Walker and C. McGavin also did the round, adding the extra Skye 'Munros' of Sgurr Dubh Mor and Sgurr Sgumain, and in August 1939, just before the outbreak of war, the feat was repeated by W. H. Murray and R. G. Donaldson who reduced the total ridge time to 19 hours. But even these exceptional feats were not the end of the story for it was argued that to make a proper job of the traverse of the main ridge and the Blaven peaks the climber should get back to his starting point within 24 hours. And this fantastic performance was eventually achieved in 1944 by that exceptional rock-climber the late J. Menlove Edwards, who did the round and returned to his starting point, Glen Brittle, in 24 hours exactly—without food caches, tents or complete knowledge of the ridge, but on his own, with a packet of sandwiches. After his ascent of Blaven and descent to Camasunary he was overtaken by darkness, but managed to continue round the coast, along the frustratingly rough track, reaching Glen Brittle at breakfast-time. Since then even faster times for the Greater Traverse, as the ridge plus Blaven and Clach Glas has been called, have been put up, but Edwards's casual approach, so typical of the man, has probably never been equalled. He didn't even carry a watch!

After all these epic feats the straightforward traverse of the Cuillin Ridge has now become almost commonplace. It has been done by grandfathers and by schoolboys, by Everest climbers and by comparative novices, and you could say that anybody, provided they can walk and climb a bit and are reasonably fit, should be able to do it. What was once considered an impossible feat within the day has now been done in about the time many people take to walk up and down Scafell Pike. Indeed, it has been said that the only distinction still remaining in this field is to push one's grandmother along the ridge in a wheelbarrow, and it is almost with shame nowadays that top climbers confess to having missed out Blaven and Clach Glas, or the peaks of Rhum across the water!

My only traverse of the ridge was in September 1959 when I had with me, as companion, my son Robin, then 19 years of age. He carried the food, the torches, the slings, the Kendal Mint Cake, the raisins and the spare sweaters. I carried the rope—unfortunately 120 feet of it, full-weight, since I hadn't a shorter length—the map, the compass and the whisky flask. Since we had spent several days on a reconnaissance of the rockier bits of the ridge, cached water at most of the right places, returned to our car which had been left at Sligachan, and broke no records, our achievement had no merit whatsoever, except that it might have been the first time the ridge had been traversed by a father and son. Our walk had been preceded by a traverse by four friends whose total ages were said to fall short of 300 years but to be considerably in excess of 200. And it was followed, the next day, by a traverse by a youngster whose time made me decide we must have been walking backwards.

Our performance was rendered even less commendable by the fact that we started from a tent pitched at the very foot of Gars-bheinn, although it could be argued that this expedient, designed to cut down the night walking, proved in the event to be much more arduous than the usual plan. We left Glen Brittle after dinner, on a glorious evening, with tent, sleeping bags, cooking stove, food and an alarm clock with the idea of getting some sleep before a night ascent of Gars-bheinn to reach the summit at dawn, but it just didn't work out that way. The alarm clock had no glass front and only one finger and therefore had to be carried most gingerly round the coast. It was also a most unreliable model so that, having pitched the tent and eaten some food, neither of us dared go off to sleep, and in fact only did so five minutes before the alarm went off. The time, if I remember rightly, was then 3.30 a.m. and, having had a cup of coffee and fastened up the tent, we set off in the darkness up the interminable screes of Gars-bheinn, feeling very tired and miserable and convinced that we had made a great mistake by our subterfuge. It would, of course, have been far better to have had a decent sleep at Glen Brittle and then walked, unencumbered, slowly round the coast and up the mountain, so that our cheating was not even worth while.

We had four small torches, all of them expendable, and we used them all in the ascent of Gars-bheinn which must be an unpleasant business at any time, but at four o'clock on the blackest of mornings is something approaching purgatory. Indeed, W. H. Murray, the well-known Scottish mountaineer, has written of an exactly similar experience on the same mountain: 'Fifteen hundred feet of perpendicular scree at midnight is a realistic foretaste of what awaits climbers in another world', and this seemed a reasonably accurate assessment. We slipped and stumbled among the rocks and boulders, just guessing at the line in the darkness, and sometimes found ourselves reduced to clawing at the sliding screes with our hands, while holding the torches in our teeth. At one point, after we had kept sliding backwards the few inches we had gained, I reminded Robin of Tilman's comment, after suffering similar indignity on a Himalayan peak, that 'Thank God, we are holding our own', and we agreed that this was our situation, too. We finally reached the summit exhausted; indeed, the only time during our traverse of the ridge when I felt really tired was at this point, immediately before the start. Fortunately, my condition increasingly improved as we went along.

The object had been to leave the summit of Gars-bheinn at dawn and this at least we achieved, although the mountains were still only grim, black precipices and the islands far below, vague shapes floating in a grey sea. But at exactly ten minutes to seven the great red ball of the sun slowly crept up behind the peak of Blaven and suddenly flooded a grey, misty world with sparkling light and dancing shadows. It was exactly the tonic we needed and we trotted on, like giants refreshed, into a long day of sunshine all the way, with a switchback of peaks ahead and, behind, the Outer Hebrides riding like great ships at anchor on the horizon.

The Thearlaich-Dubh gap went easily—a quick abseil down the short vertical side and a straightforward climb up the steep grove and slabs beyond the gap—and we made the customary visit to Sgurr Alasdair, the highest peak in the Cuillin and then carried on round the magnificent traverse of Coire Lagan. The slightly awkward slabs, unroped, down to the foot of the Sgurr Mhic Coinnich wall had to be taken carefully and we thought the toil up An Stac rather fatiguing, but we had our first excitement on the Inaccessible Pinnacle when we saw a man sitting on the top of Sgurr Dearg. So early in the morning, when most people might be having breakfast, this seemed slightly unusual, but what was even more remarkable was that he called me by name, and I saw that he was John Jackson, director of the Plas y Brenin centre in North Wales, and formerly of Kanchenjunga. I had not seen him for years and did not even know he was in this country, let alone on the same ridge in Skye. He had been camping in Glen Brittle, had heard that we were attempting the ridge—how, I can't imagine, for we thought we had kept it to ourselves—and had most kindly decided to come up and see if we wanted any oranges or mint cake instead of having his breakfast. It was a most generous and sporting gesture, completely typical of the man, and when he saw that we were well provisioned he insisted on taking the rope and rucksack and convoying us, at great speed, over the several summits of Sgurr na Banachdich before trotting down to the glen to start his own day. I suppose our acceptance of this proferred assistance should, strictly speaking, invalidate our walk as a genuine performance but we never thought about it at the time, being quite overcome by John's kindly enthusiasm. Furthermore, not content with this, he took down to the Lodge some of our useless kit, including empty flasks, informed the rest of my family that we were still alive and, surprisingly, at least one hour ahead of schedule, and left there for us, against our return, two bottles of beer. As it turned out, this most happy encounter was the only occasion all day when we saw or met anybody else.

Other encounters along the ridge I can recall were, first, of a friendly dotterel walking about on the summit rocks of Sgurr Mhic Coinnich, and secondly, a mountain hare in a little chimney on the western ridge of Sgurr nan Gillean. Both bird and animal gave us the impression they had never met human beings before. The dotterel trotted about only two yards away and then watched us from a crevice, while the mountain hare was seated on a little ledge only two feet away from my face and did not bother to move until I had studied him for fully two minutes. He then vanished into a hole at the back of the chimney nearly 3,000 feet up on a shattered rock ridge and far away from grass and heather. A friend of mine tells me he once saw a mountain hare on the same ridge—the most unlikely hide imaginable.

I have mentioned we were at least an hour ahead of schedule on Sgurr Dearg and, indeed, nearly two hours ahead at the Bhasteir Tooth, but it should be stated that this schedule had been devised to allow several stops and to take account of such possible complications as inadvertently going to sleep or being attacked by cramp or some other ailment. We had drawn up two lists of timings—our own modest schedule and Murray's timing when he did the ridge with Blaven and Clach Glas added when, we thought that, with so much further to go, he would have been taking things fairly easily. As it happened, we were also ahead of Murray's time for the Greater Traverse when we reached the Tooth but, for some reason, we made an awful meal of this problem, losing quite a lot of time, so that in the end the ridge itself took us about 12 hours—half an hour slower than Murray who still had many more hours of toil ahead of him at this point. We had climbed Naismith's Route on the Tooth two days beforehand when it was covered in slippery slime, but when we tackled it on the ridge walk, in perfectly dry conditions, we found it rather frightening and felt quite demoralized when we finally reached the top. We must have been tired by then without realizing it and it meant that we finished in only a very average sort of time whereas, with everything in our favour, we should have put up a much better performance. But, having failed to do anything remarkable, we contented ourselves with the thought that all we had really wanted to do had been to complete the ridge and see the scenery.

The traverse of the Cuillin Ridge in the day is well within the grasp of the average climber, provided he is fairly fit and able to familiarize himself with the awkward sections beforehand, and the weather is reasonable. The rock-climbing is quite straightforward but the lay-out of the ridge is a bit complicated in places—especially around Sgurr Dubh na Da Bheinn and on Bidein Druim nan Ramh—and time-wasting mistakes can easily be made in mist. If the day is likely to be very dry it is essential either to carry water or cache it beforehand, since there is no water on the ridge. Some years ago a friend of mine attempted the traverse on his own and got as far as the Bhasteir Tooth on a very hot day, but by then was so dehydrated that he had to abandon the walk and escape down Fionn Choire, practically on his hands and knees, with his tongue hanging out. He would have done the ridge with ease if he had taken the precaution of leaving a bottle of water somewhere. We attempted three caches of water but only two of them succeeded. The third, intended for Bidein Druim nan Ramh, was a bottle of water collected from the last spring in Coire na Creiche. The bottle had been found on a wall in the lane behind the Glen Brittle Lodge. I don't know what it had contained but I suspect fire-water for some time after it had been filled at the spring, the bottom of the bottle fell out in Robin's rucksack, ruining some of the contents, and that was the end of the Bidein cache. Other mistakes we made were in taking too long and heavy a rope and too much food. We left almost the whole of our food for the gulls on Bruach na Frithe after Robin had carried it for five-sixths of the ridge. Water, raisins, mint cake and glucose tablets seemed to be all that we needed. I had a swig of whisky at the same spot and this possibly contributed to our time-wasting tactics on the Tooth.

But, apart from the miseries of clawing our way up the sliding screes of Gars-bheinn in the darkness and the toe-grinding descent, at the end of the day, of Coire a' Bhasteir, we thoroughly enjoyed the walk, and the expedition ranks as one of the finest I have ever had in the mountains. We thought we saw an eagle soaring far below us near Bruach na Frithe and, in a cleft near the top of Sgurr Thormaid, we found the dwarf willow, the smallest tree in the United Kingdom, only a couple of inches high. The day grew hotter and hotter as we went along but, through the slight heat haze, we could clearly see the islands of Rhum, Canna and Eigg, far out across the dancing blue waters, although the Outer Hebrides, from Barra to Lewis, which we had earlier seen strung out along the horizon, soon disappeared. I remember the dark shapes of the hills floating in a grey sea of mist in the hour before the dawn, the golden magic of the sunrise, the rough grasp of the warm rocks as we quickly swarmed, in rubbered silence, up and down the peaks, the sense of satisfaction as we sprawled in the sunshine on the topmost rocks of Sgurr nan Gillean, the 4 miles' trudge down through the bogs to Sligachan, and the cool drink in the bar at the end.

If I ever do the ridge again—which is probably unlikely—I would start and finish at Glen Brittle, climbing down the western ridge of Sgurr nan Gillean after climbing up it, crossing over the shoulder of Am Basteir into Fionn Choire, and finishing down easy slopes to join the road through the glen. This would make a much more satisfying round, avoid the tiring descent of the Coire a' Bhasteir screes and cut out the need to leave a car at Sligachan. It was in the

Sligachan bar that we came down to earth at the end of the day. 'What about a nice sail round the coast tomorrow to pick up your tent?' asked Ron Macdonald, the boatman, completely unimpressed by our modest feat. 'Much better than wasting your time on the hills. We might get some fish.' And we did.

WINTER IN THE CAIRNGORMS

Even the reindeer seemed to find the arctic conditions trying in the Cairngorms the other day for we found them grazing disconsolately on the edge of the forest—a thousand feet lower down the mountain than their usual habitat. Higher up, on the skiing slopes, we were battling with ice, mist, blizzards and biting cold winds—all at the same time. In retrospect we might enjoy the ordeal, but at that time the reindeer seemed the sensible ones. And yet, a few days earlier atop a Lake District fell, we had been skiing in warm sunshine with not enough breeze to ripple the pools among the rocks and clear-cut views to the Scottish border and beyond. It is nearly always the same when we go up to the Highlands for the skiing—driving snow over the Drumochter, lifts closed down because of the winds, and visibility often down to a few yards—but even the worst days generally have their reward. Ours came at the end of the second day when we drove down out of the mist and blizzards to the quiet of the golden sands of Loch Morlich and the shelter of the pines of Rothiemurchus. Suddenly, within a space of 2 or 3 miles and a couple of thousand feet of lost height, we were in a new world of calm blue waters and forest glades lit by shafts of evening sunlight and gladdened by bird-song. And then, looking back at the arctic scene we had left only minutes before, we saw a remarkable sight. Through the pines and across the waters of the loch we saw the grey clouds slowly lift from the mountains like curtains at the theatre to reveal sunlit snow, smooth and shapely against a bright blue sky. Tomorrow—when we had gone—could be a glorious day.

8

Assorted Adventures

Magical Moments and Mishaps

The colours in the rich pattern of a lifetime of mountain adventure may have faded a little over the years and the fabric, in places, worn a bit thin, but here and there a few bright strands stand out to remind one of some of the highlights. But peering into the tangled weft and warp—without a diary—it seems to be not so much the big adventures I remember, but more often the little things or the things that went wrong. Days of difficult climbs satisfactorily completed or of splendid mountain walks on sunlit snow seem to merge into a pleasant haze, but days when we got lost or frightened, when some little incident or freak of weather made the expedition just a little different, are remembered. A hundred great days on Dow Crag, for instance, are forgotten, but I can recall nearly every minute of a night descent of the crag forty years ago. And my clearest memory of a dozen walks from Coniston to Scafell or Gable in the early 1930s is of one tiring return in the early hours of the morning when we finished, exhausted, in the straw of 'Daddy' Myers' barn in Langdale, among his assorted livestock. A few times, through over-confidence or carelessness, I have been lost in the Lakeland hills, although nobody was inconvenienced and I always eventually sorted out the problem for myself, but these experiences are still clearly remembered and I hope that lessons were learned. Looking back on these slightly shameful incidents I think I secretly enjoyed them as a bit of unexpected adventure—a sort of bonus to what otherwise might have been rather mundane days.

The weather, of course, has played a big part in many of these rewarding experiences in the hills, and it is true that people who only go into the mountains on fine, sunny days can miss the full flavour. It is the contrasts that matter—climbing out of the rain and mists, for instance, into a sunlit, white world, or watching the clouds suddenly torn away from the peaks after hours of drenching discomfort. One June day in 1970, in the Lakeland hills, I walked through the biggest deluge I have ever experienced—apart, perhaps, from monsoon days in Burma. Readers might have found many wet days in this book, but this was, although short, the wettest of them all—an electric storm on the Coniston fells that put down more rain in an hour than some places get in a month. For seven weeks there had been almost no measurable rain in Lakeland, with the becks silent and the fells tinder-dry, and the strange thing was that after this tremendous cloudburst the hills seemed just as dry as ever. But the really interesting part of this day was the thunder and lightning that preceded the downpour and chased me round the fells, turning an ordinary walk into something of an adventure. Even while the heavens were being rent apart they were still carting water in some of the valleys in High Furness and talking about calling in water-diviners, while an hour after the cloudburst the fells were smiling in the evening sunshine and the ground as hard and dusty as ever. The mystery was where all the water had gone, for 2½ inches of rain were said to have fallen at Chapel Stile in an hour and it was estimated that more than 5 inches had fallen in the same period at the head of the dale. Part of the Blea Tarn road was washed away and hundreds of tons of debris gouged out of the fellsides, while somebody had counted about a thousand lightning flashes in just over 4 hours.

I was doing, on my own, the time-honoured round of the Coniston fells—ten tops, if you count them all—and the slog up Wetherlam in an oppressive heat was like scrambling up the side of a gigantic Turkish bath. The last people I saw on my 12-mile walk were some boys bathing in the waterfalls of Church Beck and I met nobody else until I returned to the village some hours later. I envied the boys splashing about in the water for, although I was stripped to the waist, the perspiration was pouring off my head and face in a constant stream, my rucksack seemed glued to my back, and the air so heavy you felt you were walking through blankets. As I toiled higher the air became even more oppressive and the heat haze closed in around me until I could hardly see Tilberthwaite. And then, just before reaching my first summit, the thunder that had been growling in the distance for some time suddenly exploded a few miles away to the north and the first lightning flashes stabbed across the sky. But from the top of Wetherlam the Lakeland fells, from the dark trough of Wrynose Bottom to the jagged line of the Scafells, looked more like a scene from Dante's Inferno. The heat haze had been transformed into a boiling cauldron of cloud with dark pillars of mist reaching to the sky and grey whirlpools of vapour swirling above the valleys. It looked infinitely menacing and I was wondering whether anybody was in the middle of it when, suddenly, the lightning cracked immediately overhead and the thunder seemed to rock the mountain top. At last I was beginning to enjoy myself; how much better was all this noise and tumult than crawling through the Turkish bath lower down. I continued on to the secondary summit of Black Sails, nearly a mile away, with the lightning flashing and the thunder rolling all round, but it was not until I was descending into the gap of Swirl Hause before the ascent of Prison Band that the fury of the storm really exploded.

The lightning jagged down from the heavens, first just ahead of me and then just behind me, until I was convinced that Jove was sitting up above with his thunderbolts trying to get my range. One particularly vicious flash struck the rocks about 50 yards behind me and a sheep, quietly cropping the turf, suddenly exploded into life and ran, helter-skelter, across the fellside, baa—ing piteously. And a raven, sailing past the crags, fled croaking wildly to the south. It was possible to judge, more or less, where the lightning was striking and, on the optimistic assumption that lightning only strikes the same place once, I kept hurrying on to try to reach these places in time, although realizing, of course, that the chances of being hit were really very remote indeed. The thunder was deafening, the air full of noise and flashes, and each clap of thunder echoed round the crags like a drumroll, but it was fascinating rather than frightening and, in any case, there was nothing I could do about it.

And then, on the top of Great Carrs, I saw the mothballs, rolling along the ground ahead of me as if they had dropped out of my pockets, and a moment later things started dropping on my head and back. They were, of course, hailstones, the size, shape and colour of mothballs, and soon there were thousands of them dropping out of the sky and rolling down the fellside towards Seathwaite Tarn. An hour before I had been sweltering in oppressive heat, and now pieces of ice were falling out of the sky, and the air was suddenly chilled. Later, in the valley, I learned that the shade temperature had dropped in minutes from 81 degrees Fahrenheit to 61 degrees. After traversing the two little peaks of Carrs I walked up Grey Friar and had my sandwiches by the cairn, sitting in the middle of the storm, and it was not until I was on my way back to Great How Crags that the really heavy rain began. All the way along the ridge and then on to Brim Fell, Coniston Old Man, Dow Crag and Buck Pike the deluge continued and I was soon soaked through to the skin and my boots filled with water. The rain really did seem to be coming down in stair-rods, right out of the east, but, remarkably, the ground soaked it up immediately, and the familiar squelching through Lakeland bog in heavy rain was absent. To the east the sky was a great black curtain and inches of rain must have fallen in that hour. I have rarely seen such menace in the sky as I saw that day, and the rain was so heavy and the ground so hard that the water seemed to be bouncing up around my knees. Once wet through it was pleasant enough and the scrambling up streaming rocks a welcome change from the dusty toil earlier in the day.

I carried on over Brown Pike and down to the Walna Scar track where, all at once, the sun came out and I tried to dry myself out near the old familiar stones of Cove Bridge. The larks were singing as I came down the track to Coniston where the early evening looked just as hot and sunny as it had been for weeks. I remembered, as I came down the track across Little Arrow Moor, a June day ten years earlier when I had walked down the same path from Dow Crag in a thunderstorm that had transformed a dusty, dried-up landscape into a tilted swamp, alive with a hundred rivers, and a hot, sultry afternoon had become an inferno of noise and fury. But this time, remarkably enough, there were no new becks rushing down the fellside—just the same, dried-up watercourses and the tarns as low as ever. All these inches of rain had been swallowed up by the bone-dry ground, and half an hour after the worst storm in Lakeland for many years, you just couldn't tell there'd been any rain at all.

The weather has provided many other memorable experiences in the hills including the sight of four Brocken Spectres, those remarkable mountain apparitions that used to strike not a little terror into the imaginations of the early climbers. Nowadays, the

Sgurr Mhic Coinnich from Coir' an Lochain

Sgurr nan Gillean and the Ridge

Brocken Spectre is dismissed as a simple reflection phenomenon, caused by the shadow of the observer being cast on to the mist or fog by sunlight, but it is the apparent size of the figure that makes its appearance, to those seeing it for the first time, so remarkable and even alarming. The giant, apparently striding the peaks miles away and obeying every step and movement of the observer, is really only a life-size shadow; the eerie colossus is an illusion. Three of my Brocken Spectres were seen when I was with others, once in Scotland, on the hills, above Glen Shiel, so that the first time there was comfort and confirmation in company, but the fourth occasion was by far the most dramatic sighting, and I was alone on Bowfell. There he was, a gigantic, ghostly figure, looking about 50 feet high and standing in the mist on the edge of the ridge that looked down on Stake Pass. And behind the figure, throwing it into high relief, were ringed concentric circles of gold, blue and red, as if the heavens were on fire, and for a moment the earth seemed to stand still in wonder at the glory of the vision. But this colossus striding the heavens was no wrath of God nor even a Lakeland version of the Grey Man of Ben Macdhui but, by now, merely an old friend. I raised my arm and the apparition, apparently standing on the ridge a mile away, raised his; I climbed upwards into the mist and the vision did the same.

It was on a strangely quiet February day in 1971, up to then a remarkably mild and snow-free winter, that I saw this my last Brocken Spectre—a calm, balmy, sunny day sandwiched between other days of clammy hill-fog that had been hanging over the district, on and off, for weeks. But that morning in the head of Langdale the farmers were manuring the fields and river-board men were working in the beck in the sunshine. The smoke rose straight in the air from the farmhouse chimneys, it was warm enough to walk without sweater or anorak, and huge, white, billowy clouds hung motionless about the mountain tops. Patches of snow could be seen peeping through the clouds on Crinkle Crags while aircraft carved their vapour trails in the clear blue sky above the Pikes. I went into the clouds somewhere above the top of The Band and it was high on the rocky east ridge of Bowfell, not far below the summit, that I saw the Spectre. The white clouds were patchy at this point and when crossing the top of one of the gullies I noticed a movement or shadow on my right and, stopping, saw the Spectre clearly outlined, through the mist, on a distant ridge. The sun was shining through the fleecy clouds above the Crinkles which were exactly behind me and the image appeared to be photographed on to the thin mist across the upper reaches of Mickleden. The circular rainbow behind the apparently huge figure, striding the skies, was much more spectacular than in other Brocken Spectres I remembered. In effect, there seemed to be three different rainbow rings within each other, making a kaleidoscope of colour. For some time the apparition marched with me over the fells but then it disappeared as I went up towards the summit, across hard patches of snow, glistening in the sunlight. There was nobody on top—I saw nobody on the hills all day—and the familiar view from the summit was quite breathtaking. From my perch I looked down rocks and snow patches towards Langdale and Langstrath on one side and distant Dunnerdale on the other but the mountains, all around the horizon, were hidden beneath a sea of fleecy white cloud that filled the head of the dales. But here and there, around the compass, tiny islands of grass and rock—the highest mountain tops—floated on the white sea below the bluest of skies and the sun beat down on the snow as it does in the Alps in the spring. I sat up there for half an hour, identifying the distant spikes of rock and enjoying the sunshine, and then trotted down to the frozen pools of Three Tarns and along the Crinkles for home. At the end of the ridge I left the sunlight and came down the shadowed ravines in Oxendale to the intake fields, feeling I had stolen a rare day and a rewarding visitation, and for several days afterwards the Lakeland hills were cloaked in damp mist with nothing—not even a Brocken Spectre—to be seen.

Sometimes, in the autumn, there is a magical quality of the lighting in the fells, a strange, almost ethereal diffusion of colours and shapes that seems to speak of long, lost summers and the cold breath of approaching winter. Almost as if the mountains were being metamorphosed into a fairyland of alpine dimensions. One year, on the Napes Ridges, I saw the effect in particularly striking form when the lighting seemed to transform the crags into tremendous precipices, disappearing through orange-tinted vapours into unseen depths. Instead of being on the Arrowhead we could have been on the Peteret Ridge or the Grepon and there seemed no means of judging the depths below, even though we could dimly see the screes through the thin mists. Some years later I had much the same feeling of yawning gulfs and immense distances on a simple walk over Brim Fell when returning over the tops after a day on Dow Crag—an extraordinary lighting effect that made the innocent ridges above Low Water look like the Brenva face of Mont Blanc and turned the grassy summit plateau into a tightrope walk for the gods. The transformation seemed to be caused by a combination of several factors—the new autumn nip in the air, a complete absence of wind and the presence of extremely thin cloud through which the late afternoon sun shone in a lazy, haphazard way. The colours, orange predominating, were as striking as when the Brocken Spectre makes its appearance and, no doubt, the requirements for the two phenomena are similar. All the way down the ridge to Levers Water we remained in this strange, magical world, with figures on nearby slopes thrown into curious relief and looking as if they were miles away. While later, down at the tarn, with the surface completely mirroring the crags, we might have been on the edge of some great African lake with shores reaching far beyond the horizon —just the sort of place, someone romantically suggested, where King Arthur had sailed away on his funeral pyre to Avalon.

Mountaintop views above a sea of white clouds are among the special bonuses we can win from the hills. In an earlier book* I have written of a youthful visit to Scafell to see the sunrise when we had this experience, and later, soon after dawn, saw the mountains of Scotland, Wales, and Ireland from the summit. And from exactly the same spot, more than forty years later, I enjoyed the same view of cottonwool clouds across the whole of Lakeland, although the more remarkable distant view never materialized a second time. A few years ago a man in Hertfordshire who had read about my sighting of England, Scotland, Ireland and Wales from the same mountain-top wrote to me of his own experience. He told me he had been walking across the Carneddau from Llyn Ogwen to Aber one November morning in 1967 and from the summit of Carnedd Llewelyn had had what he described as the view of a lifetime. He went on: 'We could see Ireland, the Isle of Man, the whole of Wales spread out like a map with the Bristol Channel glinting beyond and, to the north, the Pennines. Then, further to the north, we saw two or three peaks sticking up out of the sea—very small, but absolutely clear—and my friend said that one of them was Scafell. It was 11.30 in the morning, crystal-clear air, frosty and the first snows of the Welsh winter down to about 3,350 feet.' And this seemed

* *In Mountain Lakeland* (1963).

welcome confirmation of our 1929 sighting, from the top of Scafell at about six o'clock in the morning, of Snowdonia.

My second 'sea of cloud' view from the top of Scafell came on a walk over the roof of England by way of the long southern ridge out of Eskdale. The view came from near the cairn with the ceiling of the clouds at about 3,000 feet, so that the whole of the Lake District was completely buried in cotton wool, the only islands being the top of Scafell where I was standing, the upper rocks of Scafell Pinnacle and, a mile away, the summit of Scafell Pike, the highest point in England. I could see half a dozen figures, like matchsticks, standing on the distant cairn, but nobody and nothing else anywhere below, not a tree or a river or a farm or even a boulder. Everything in the north-west of England—or so it appeared—was below the clouds and only the people on top of the Pike and myself were above them in the sunshine. For the previous two hours I had been toiling up, in oppressive heat below leaden skies, with only occasional glimpses of thin sunlight but now, above the clouds, the air was suddenly crisp and cold and the sunlight dazzling. In a few minutes I had climbed out of a sticky autumn day into an alpine spring. Once again the top of the clouds stretching to above the horizon in all directions was perfectly level—a sparkling white sea glowing in the sunshine pouring down from unbroken blue skies. No doubt it was a pleasant enough day in the valleys of Lakeland but above 3,000 feet it was a magical day—with perhaps only seven people enjoying it. But it was too chilly, even in the autumn sunshine, to sit up there long and soon I had to descend into the clouds again. Broad Stand was greasy and the track down the scree slopes below Mickledore rather slippery but, below the clouds, the long trough of Eskdale was a miracle of evening beauty, the fells lit by a purple glow and the intake fields alive with the sounds of sheep.

One year when I saw two Brocken Spectres, walked dry-foot across a mountain tarn in October, and met a man with an umbrella on the top of Scafell Pike, perhaps the most memorable and unusual experience came on Christmas Eve. The previous day had been wet and misty but at night a particularly severe frost quickly converted the roads into skating rinks and gripped the fells in an iron fist so that Christmas Eve was heralded with a remarkable dawn. From my house I watched a huge yellow sun slowly rise above the fells around New Hutton and, within a quarter of an hour, the sunshine had melted the morning mists, flooding the fields with golden light. There was not one wisp of cloud in the whole of the heavens and not a breath of wind. I left for the hills with skis, ice-axe, crampons and a shovel—in case of difficulty on the roads—but, although there was snow and ice on Kirkstone Pass, there were no problems. The view of the Coniston and Langdale fells from the Ings to Troutbeck road was dramatic—the hills, lightly dusted with new snow, showing razor-sharp beneath the bright blue sky and the whole of the Windermere valley buried in a sea of white cloud. I have often felt rather sorry for people living around the shore of England's largest lake who, on many mornings in the year, never see the sun that may be shining brightly only a few hundred feet above their chimneys. Indeed, when I returned over Kirkstone this particular Christmas Eve after about six hours in the sunshine, the Windermere valley was still cloaked in white cloud and, for all I knew, might have been like this all day. It was warm work, in shirt-sleeves, walking up the fells from Glenridding in the hot sunshine although the ground was frozen as hard as rock and I soon decided that a walk round the tops would be preferable, on such a superb day, to skiing in the shade on rutted ice. The view of Keswick, the Thirlmere valley and the western fells from the summit of Raise was as magnificent as I have ever seen. The dales were filled with the bright orange light you often see on clear winter days, the hills stretched to the horizon in successive ridges of gradually darkening blue, while long, fish-shaped wisps of white cloud, looking as if they had been stuck on a child's model with glue, hung about 1,000 feet above the valleys. And, in the very zenith of the firmament, an unseen jet aircraft traced a sparkling white vapour trail across the blue, like a scratch on ice.

It was on the short, icy pull up to Helvellyn Low Man that I saw the balloon. It was hanging stationary above the snow-covered ridge of Swirrel Edge—a beautiful blue sphere, darker than the sky, glinting in the sunlight. At first I thought it was some sort of small meteorological balloon, something to do with mountain rescue perhaps, held down by a cord on the Edge, but when I realized it was more than half a mile away, directly over Red Tarn, I could see it was a really big balloon, with men on board. Balloons had flown over the Lake District before, mostly on publicity trips, but this was the first time I had ever seen one in the hills, and the situation for observing the balloon—and equally, I should think, for looking out from it—could hardly have been more fortunate and dramatic. The cornices of frozen snow stood out for about 12 feet from the ridge of Helvellyn and, standing on the edge, I was exactly level with the balloon, as it hung motionless above the serrated saddle on Swirrel Edge, with the High Street fells as backcloth behind. One remarkable feature was that although the wind, blowing out of the south, was now quite strong on the top of Helvellyn, the balloon remained still, perhaps held in the thermals rising from Red Tarn. However, after a time, it moved very slowly south, finally passing only about 30 to 50 feet above the summit of Catstycam on which I could see three or four tiny figures who were, no doubt, within speaking distance of the balloonists. I watched the balloon for about a quarter of an hour and saw it almost graze the summit of Raise and drop down over the east side of Stybarrow Dodd. Later I learned that the balloon had been from Holker Hall near Cark in Cartmel and that a projected flight up the dales in southern Lakeland had got slightly out of hand, taking the balloonists over one of the highest ranges in the district and many miles away from their planned route. The balloon eventually came down in the foothills near Threlkeld after what must have been an exciting, if unpremeditated, journey. To float silently just above the snow-capped hills of Lakeland on one of the most perfect days of the year, with every feature of the fells showing clearly just beneath the basket—and not thousands of feet below, as from an aircraft—must be a remarkably rewarding way to spend a day out. Just to watch this colourful runaway on Christmas Eve, so close and in such fortuitous circumstances of weather, was certainly a memorable experience for me, and as I rattled down Striding Edge I quietly envied the balloonists their good fortune.

Nights out in the Lakeland fells can be pleasant enough if planned and should not be disastrous if unpremeditated, although to be avoided in winter-time. On a clear and, ideally, a moonlight night the fells can often be easily traversed, even without a torch, although torches should obviously always be taken if there is any risk of a night out. Fortunately, most of my nights in the hills have been planned and the other experiences taught me lessons at the cost of no more than a little inconvenience and discomfort to myself, and to nobody else. Others have not been so fortunate but some experience and common sense can normally save one from the worst effects of a night out in the hills. To walk the hills at night, when all sounds, except the noise of the becks and the rustle of the wind in the crags, are stilled is a worthwhile experience, and a night in a sleeping bag in the heather is no discomfort and can be a luxury in summertime. I remember a midnight traverse of Striding Edge in the moonlight that was as safe and easy as a daytime walk but twice as exhilarating, and several dawns in the high fells with views that you never see on the picture postcards. Even familiar countryside is transformed in the early morning for the shadows are coming from an unusual direction and places rarely seen illuminated appear strangely different. While a planned night out on the fells—instead of sleeping at home—gives you the feeling, as you trot down for breakfast, that you have stolen an extra day. I have spent the night, or part of it, on most of the bigger Lakeland mountains and have learned something new on every occasion. Unpremeditated nights out might have been slightly uncomfortable at the time, but, in retrospect, amusing. At the beginning of this chapter I mentioned a day on Great Gable that lasted until the next morning. This was just bad management but I don't regret the experience. Besides, we were young and took these things in our stride.

Two of us had walked from Coniston to Great Gable by way of Fell Foot and Esk Hause to do some climbing. It was a perfect day and, after we had been up and down most of the Napes Ridges, we both felt loath to leave for the long walk back and so did some more climbs on Kern Knotts. It was beginning to grow dark when we finally decided to leave but we were pretty fit and tough in those days and, as we both had torches in our rucksacks, were not perturbed. But, on the walk from Styhead to Esk Hause, both the torches petered out and we found ourselves in inky darkness, with even the path invisible. I remember we took stock of the situation somewhere near Angle Tarn, where we had a meal and speculated whether to go on or stay put. We could not see the tarn but calculated we were in that area. Our compasses gave us a rough direction but that was all. The darkness was complete and impenetrable. In the end we decided to continue our journey since activity, on such a chilly night, seemed preferable to an enforced bivouac and we believed we knew every inch of the way. But the descent of Rossett Gill, in the darkness, proved a nightmare. When you have been up and down this place several times in daylight you might think you know it fairly well but, under these conditions, we had to explore every yard as we slipped, crashed into boulders and stumbled, sightless, down the zigzags. A direct descent would have been much easier but, having to feel our way, we found it as tricky and complicated as descending a glacier. We put on the rope for we kept falling down short, rocky pitches, and took it in turns to take the lead in finding the way down. How many hours it took us to get down to the sheepfold I can't remember but I know we were both pretty exhausted when we reached the level turf of Mickleden and found the easy section to Middlefell Farm extremely trying. By then we had decided we must get some sleep—it might have been four or five o'clock in the morning—and when we reached Wall End at the foot of Blea Tarn pass we stumbled into the hay in 'Daddy' Myers' barn, and dozed off immediately. We awoke a few hours later to find ourselves surrounded by livestock, including a horse, some sheep and several hens but, after a wash in the beck, felt completely refreshed and presented ourselves to the farmer with a request for breakfast. This was provided in the stone-flagged kitchen—I think he took a shilling or two for breakfast but nothing for the 'bed'—and we went on our way rejoicing after a long day and night on our feet that must have lasted something like 20 hours. But, like our wet and windy traverse of High Street and my storm adventure on the Coniston fells, this had been one of the good days.

Another night adventure from our climbing hut at Coniston, which I remember as clearly as if it had happened last week, provided further proof that some nights can be quite incredibly dark. We had been climbing on Dow Crag and, as usual, being keen and energetic, had left things late. It was getting dark quickly but we decided the quickest way off the crag was to come down Blizzard Chimney, this being the more direct route. But halfway down the chimney we were overtaken by darkness and, although we knew the climb very well, found we could neither see nor feel the holds. It seemed darker towards the foot of the chimney and in Easter Gully than it was higher up the crag, so we climbed back up the chimney on to Easy Terrace. By this time it was completely dark and we could not see our hands in front of our faces. We kept on the rope and progressed along the Terrace, one at a time on our seats. It was impossible even to see the outline of the crag against the sky; everything was completely black. To the left of the Terrace there is a sheer drop to the screes and, of course, we were aware of this. As a slight guide we scratted about in a sitting posture, trying to find

The ridges of Blencathra

Coniston Old Man ridge from Swirl Hause

Carlin Gill in the Howgills

Walkers on Stony Cove Pike

The track through Kentmere

Sharp Edge on Blencathra

bits of loose stone, and these we threw gently to our left. If we heard them drop a few feet away we knew we were all right and still on the Terrace; if we heard nothing or a distant clatter down the crag we were too near the edge. Several times we fell down the pitches on the Terrace—you don't notice them in daylight—but we were always held by the rope and came to no harm, apart from a few scratches. It was rather a nerve-racking but exciting descent of Easy Terrace. Perhaps it was the first roped descent, too. Even when we reached the foot of the crag there was no opportunity to relax for we had yet to reach the cave among the boulders where the rucksacks containing the torches had been left. To get a clue as to the direction of the cave we literally felt our way along the foot of the crag until we recognized, with our fingers, the rocky groove that is the first pitch of Abraham's Route on B Buttress. We knew then that we were more or less directly above the cave and were able to find our way down to it and our torches. This time they did not let us down and we were soon down at our hut on the shore of Coniston Water—hours late but none the worse for our little adventure.

Many people with long experience of the hills will confess, if they are honest, that there have been occasions when they have been lost. Not so seriously that they have had to call out the search teams, but temporarily lost for an hour or two, and perhaps even coming down into the wrong valley. They have not been proud of these incidents, but, providing they have not caused anxiety to anybody else, have not particularly regretted them. For to be lost in the hills when the weather conditions are not serious can, for the experienced mountaineer or hill-walker, be little worse than a light-hearted adventure—something to spice what might otherwise have been a fairly ordinary sort of day. After all, to walk the hills in fine weather on tracks that have been in use for up to a hundred years is hardly an adventure for people who have probably been the same way many times before. Rock-climbing standards have soared remarkably in recent years but fell walkers mostly use the same tracks that the Victorians pioneered, so that the possibility of adventure, even of the mildest sort, is remote—unless the weather changes. And a bit of adventure, something that stamps the day as a little different from the others, is what most of us seek in the hills, whether we are pioneering new rock-climbs or doing a modest round of familiar fells. So we run into a freak storm, or see a Brocken Spectre or a balloon, or rescue a cragfast sheep or explore an old mine or just get lost for an hour or two, and the day is made.

Let me emphasize that I am writing about experienced people getting lost—inexperienced folk should take more care. Experienced climbers and walkers who get lost in the hills in reasonable weather should be able to sort things out for themselves and escape with a soaking, a longer walk than anticipated, or a late return to the valley. But every precaution should be taken against getting lost in bad or winter weather, or in unfamiliar country. Outside the Lake District I take much greater care with map and compass and I should hate to be lost in some of the remote parts of Scotland. But in my homeland hills I am, I am afraid, much too casual and over-confident. How could I possibly get lost, even in the worst conditions, on the Helvellyn range or in the Northern Pennines, I have probably thought to myself, but in fact I have been lost in both of these areas. Five of us, two well-known Himalayan mountaineers, two distinguished rock-climbers and myself, once got lost on Kirk Fell. We had been climbing on Boat Howe Crag and at the end of the day, in thick mist, decided to return to Wasdale by walking over the summit. Each one of us claimed to know the mountain and its two summits like the back of his hand but after a couple of hours of fruitless wanderings in all directions, with all of us taking the lead in turn, we were still defeated and, in the end, only made the valley by walking downhill and, of course, coming down on the wrong side of the mountain. We had to pay for our over-confidence by an extra ration of walking when we were rather tired.

This was, I think, my first discovery that it is easier to walk in circles in mist than in a straight line. On another occasion I was skiing down from Raise on my own along a route I must have taken dozens of times when I took a wrong turning and suddenly found myself completely lost. Very foolishly, and because I thought that if I knew any Lakeland mountain in winter it was Raise, I had left far too late for the valley. The mist was thick and it was snowing and when I took the wrong turning it was nearly dark. Many foolish mistakes were made that evening and I paid for them. Once I found myself on unfamiliar ground I should have followed my ski tracks back uphill to see where I had gone wrong but, instead, I kept on down steepening slopes until I ran into rocks, vertical juniper and deep pockets of soft snow into which I fell, at intervals, up to my armpits. By then, of course, I was carrying my skis and it was quite dark and rather frightening. In daylight, this sort of thing, when skiers who have gone off-route find themselves involved in minor mountaineering, is described as 'bird's nesting' and looked upon as a slightly humorous and undignified situation. My predicament, on the craggy, lower slopes of Raise at night, was certainly undignified but the humour of it escaped me at the time and I was extremely relieved when I finally emerged from the clouds, battered and soaked through, to see the distant lights of Glenridding. Again, the whole thing was inexcusable and rank bad mountaineering, but perhaps I learned some lessons.

But there was another occasion when I got myself temporarily lost while skiing when I was unlucky rather than stupid. It was in the northern Pennines and I had loaned my compass to a friend who was doing a ski traverse over Cross Fell while I, rather restricted by my dog Sambo who could only make slow going in deep snow, decided to ski on the east side of Great Dun Fell. At the end of the day I was skiing down very familiar ground to the car when I ran into a complete white-out with thick mist and driving snow that blotted out ski tracks within seconds. Sambo, plastered in snow except for his eyes, soon became invisible and, with constant turning round to find him and my tracks disappearing almost immediately, I found it extremely difficult to keep direction. It seems incredible, in country that I know so well, that this should have happened, but after a while I realized that I did not know where I was. Visibility in the blizzard was no more than a couple of yards and I kept losing Sambo. It was also growing dark. With a compass I could have struck the right line but, without one, I finally decided to strike uphill for the radio station on the summit and then ski easily down the road. This, I thought, would be simple but it proved extremely difficult. I would start uphill only to find, after a few yards, that I was merely climbing a hillock and so would try in another direction to come up with the same result. On my own it would have been easier, but with the dog it was just frustrating, and for a long time we must have wandered in the blizzard and the oncoming darkness over quite an area of the northern Pennines without getting anywhere. In the end, of course, things sorted themselves out for I managed to pick out a post, nearly buried in the snow, which eventually led me, in the darkness, to the mountain road, but it had been a chastening experience. Some years later an experienced mountaineer was lost in a white-out in the same area, finally turning up in the Garrigill area, miles away, after the search teams had been alerted. White-outs with nothing but white on the ground and in the sky, and visibility reduced to nil, provide some of the worst winter conditions in the hills and careful compass-work is necessary. Once I met these conditions on the Helvellyn ridge when a simple traverse of the most familiar walk in the Lakeland hills became almost an expedition. Subconsciously, we are always hoping for adventure in the hills and we remember the tough days of storm and cloud when the sunny days are all forgotten. And if adventure doesn't come our way we seek it out if we are young.

One of our little ploys before the war, when we were young and fit, was to make it a point of honour to bathe in a lake or tarn every weekend—no matter what time of the year. Mostly, these excruciatingly invigorating performances were achieved in Coniston Water from our hut on the shore of the lake but we also often bathed in Goats Water at the foot of Dow Crag, on at least one occasion breaking thin ice to do so. In the summer these dips were enjoyed, but in winter-time it was just a case of gritting your teeth, flopping in and then scrambling out as quickly as possible, with honour satisfied. I suppose we got inured to it but it makes me shiver now just to think of it. Nowadays, I can still enjoy a surreptitious tarn bathe on a warm summer's day, but even in August these mountain bathes can sometimes be almost too invigorating. The coldest summer bathe I can remember was in Hard Tarn, underneath Nethermost Pike—a perfect mountain pool but too often out of the sunshine.

Another youthful adventure, often enjoyed on days when the crags were out of condition, was to explore old mine workings with ropes and torches. We used to rope down rickety shafts and explore flooded galleries and caves, but were careful to employ normal safety techniques and never came to any harm. Once we got into one of Lanty Slee's caves in an old quarry in the fells above the Brathay and found the remains of his fires where he had his still for making whisky out of potatoes. We discovered bits of old cask hoops and other evidence of the trade that went on in those hills more than a hundred years ago, and we even found an underground store—regrettably empty. Years later I met Lanty's son, Adam, who lived to be more than 100, and he told me quite a lot about his famous father—the only Lake District smuggler and whisky maker who has gone down in history. Lanty Slee's cave is now blocked up, but the explorer with proper tackle and rock-climbing experience can still spend interesting hours in seeking out the ways of the old miners and quarrymen—a brave, tough breed who worked with incredible courage, patience and ingenuity, and the most elementary and often dangerous equipment, burrowing into the hills to satisfy the greed of their masters.

On other days when the clouds were down or the rocks too wet and slimy we used to go beck scrambling, a practice I have continued, although not so adventurously as years ago, until the present day. You simply follow a beck to its source, climbing the waterfalls or, when these defeat you, the rock walls at the side, and the opportunities and permutations are almost unlimited—except by one's lack of skill. Two of us once descended Tilberthwaite Gill in this way—down the waterfalls, over the pools, across the walls and in and out of caves, carefully avoiding the ladders and bridges that in those days made a sort of staging up the ravine. We had a lot of fun and got very wet but it transformed what might have been a very ordinary day into quite an exciting one. You can either pick your becks from the map, using them as new routes up familiar fells, or select them on the ground, and the scrambling can vary from simple leaping across boulders to difficult climbs up water-worn rocks, with the beck pouring down your sleeves and out of your boots, and the fear of a cold dip in the pool below to spur you on. We used to get several duckings but nowadays I circumvent the nasty places. Almost always on these little expeditions the river scenery is delightful and you often make height very easily, apparently without effort, so interesting is the work. Every few minutes you turn a corner or top a pitch to see new scenery ahead, and the noise of the water and the thrill of finding the right route generally combine to make a fascinating ascent, especially on a warm day. Sometimes a beck will start in the valley as a lazy river, become a necklace of tumbling waterfalls higher up, and finish under the summit crags as a tiny spring trickling out of the boulders. To follow these becks from the dale to their source can often be a piece of pure exploration, for few people will have been there before, and you are often discovering 'new' country.

This is the real joy of adventuring in the Lakeland fells—finding new ways up. It could be said that a man who has been up nearly all the Lakeland fells, but only by the well-marked tracks, may not really know his mountains and might be surprised—or even lost—

if taken half a mile away from the tracks he knows so well. There is beauty and interest in walking familiar fells in summer-time but no challenge; to get something more rewarding out of the mountains you need to tackle them in winter or in bad weather, but you can also get a great deal of pleasure by seeking new ways to the top, away from the tracks. Rock-climbers, for instance, can find the most difficult way to the summit by linking up the small crags and outcrops—there is quite a challenging route to Pillar Rock from the Liza, using rock nearly all the way, while Red Pike throws down a similar challenge into upper Mosedale. Indeed, nearly every Lake District mountain runs to rock on at least one side and you can often select routes, far away from tracks, that can be anything from modest scrambles to moderately challenging ascents. The Scafell Pike area abounds with possibilities and other mountains worthy of exploration away from the tracks include Crinkle Crags, Hart Crag, Fairfield, Nethermost Pike, Red Screes, Blencathra, Wetherlam, Base Brown and many more. In time, the adventurous walker will learn that places are often much easier than they look, but he will also learn judgement, which is the most important aspect of mountaineering. The north-west ridge of Catstycam, for instance, can look quite tricky but is really a very easy walk, while the craggy steps of Greenhow End provide an interesting way up Fairfield. There is also an interesting rocky route across the side of Hart Crag above Deepdale, another up Red Screes from the top of Kirkstone Pass, the rocky front of Grasmoor above Crummock Water, a route up Harrison Stickle by way of the ravine of Dungeon Ghyll, and many possibilities at the head of Eskdale. For a change, you can even walk round a mountain instead of over it, keeping, if you like, along the same contour, say 2,000 feet. I once walked round Grey Friar in this way and, although rather tiring on the ankles, the little trip took me into several new places and showed me slightly different scenery.

And so many Lake District mountains are curiously neglected. Sheffield Pike is one, Seatallan another and Ullscarf a third, while the summit of Lingmell, one of the best viewpoints in the whole of Lakeland, is comparatively rarely visited. Lingmell boasts the most splendidly sited and beautiful summit cairn in the district—when it is not decapitated by vandals—but there is no other evidence of the hand of man up there, no piles of old tins and orange peel, and not even a track across the top. Few people bother to go on to

Lingmell because it is so close to the highest mountains in England and just off the popular highway, but it is one of the most superb grandstands in the country. No other Lake District mountain is more closely ringed with rock and scree, and the view of Great Gable across the great trough of Wasdale must be the most detailed sight of one mountain's architecture in the national park. From just north of the cairn on Lingmell you appear to be looking right across the dale at the district's most shapely mountain as through a telephoto lens or a zoom camera. Every feature of Gable leaps into sharp focus—you can easily pick out the Needle on a good day—and you have the impression of tremendous depths below your feet. And, as if this was not enough, Lingmell also happens to display, sliced into its eastern flank, the biggest ravine in the district—the dog-legged Piers Gill, large enough to hide an army; while the longest rock-climb on any of our crags, the 2,000 feet-high Pilgrim's Progress, leads out of the Gill to the top of the mountain. All this on the mountain the crowds don't notice—a mountain for the connoisseur. And there are several more of them, and hundreds of 'new' ways to the top, all waiting to be sought out on days when there are processions on Striding Edge and Styhead as busy as the High Street.

THE RIGHT PLACE

Among the best places to visit on the right sort of day are the rocky coves scooped out of the east face of the Helvellyn range. While scores of people are walking the rather uninteresting summit ridge or scrambling along the well-trodden tracks over Striding and Swirrel Edges the corries, largely trackless and, except for the tinkling of becks, quiet as a cathedral, can be quite deserted. You can see the walkers on the ridges, small as matchsticks, but they probably can't see you, swallowed up in the wilderness of rock, bracken and grass, and the craggy fellsides shut you off from the bustle of the most popular mountain in the district, even in high summer. The best time is the morning, with the sunlight flooding the coves and highlighting the eastern crags, but the rewards can be enjoyed in any month of the year. A bright morning in spring, with the longest lasting snows in the district reaching down into the corries and the ice glistening in the gullies would be my favourite, but last weekend was a fair substitute. The waterfalls in Ruthwaite Beck were in noisy spate as I left the main track through the valley but the silence by Hard Tarn was only broken by the croak of the ravens as they tumbled across the sky. Hard Tarn, an oval jewel caught on a rock ledge just below the topmost crags, is one of the least-visited tarns in the district. The other day it reflected all the colours of the hills and the sky—an upland miniature of Lanty Tarn, down among the Scots pines near Grassthwaite How, which we passed a couple of hours later before returning to civilization by the Grisedale Beck.

Buttermere from Rannerdale Knotts

St Sunday Crag from Boredale Hause

Approaching Sharp Edge

9

How Many Mountains?

Some Scope for Exploration

Peak-bagging in the Lake District is hardly the recognized sport it is among the Munro-studded mountains of Scotland. Few people, after a day's wandering over the Lakeland fells, go home and tick off their ascents against a printed list as they do in Scotland, for there just aren't any lists—apart from a few private ones. And the average mountain-walker, who may well know there are 277 'Munros' in Scotland, might have little idea of the number of fells in the Lake District, nor greatly care about the matter. Lakeland hills, we say, are there to be enjoyed and not just ticked off, and peak-bagging is a Scottish disease.

It is, of course, realized that you can hardly talk about Scottish mountains and Lakeland mountains in the same breath since you could hide all the Cumbrian fells in one corner of the Highlands. And the Scottish hills are much higher. There are 545 'tops' in Scotland more than 3,000 feet in height and 277 of these are 'Munros' or separate 3,000-feet mountains. But in little Lakeland there are only seven 3,000-feet 'tops' and only four of these would have qualified for Sir Hugh Munro's accolade if he had bothered to pursue his investigations south of the Border and listed the hills he found. So that, on this basis, there seems little scope for peak-bagging in Lakeland, even if we were tempted into it, and we content ourselves with trotting round the '3,000s' while the super men try to run up and down forty, fifty or sixty tops in the day.

But although peak-bagging in Lakeland, for its own sake, may seem hardly worth while, the ordinary fell-walker can get a little quiet satisfaction by studying his maps and seeing if he has really explored all the high ground. He may well discover, even if he thinks he has been over all the mountains, that there are many heights he has not trodden, and to seek these out, as casually as may be, will at least take him into new places. The dyed-in-the-wool peak-bagger may deplore this casual approach but I commend it. You don't decide to polish off all the Lakeland tops as you might embark on the Munros for you probably don't know how many there are, and you've not heard of anybody else doing it. You just get out your maps and when you have noted the untrodden tops you might go so far as to decide that when you are next in the Buttermere fells, for example, you might continue along the ridge to Great Borne which you don't remember having done before. Or you might notice some unfamiliar fells at the back of Skiddaw and earmark them for some winter's day when the rocks are out of condition, or there's no ice in the gullies or not enough snow for skiing.

Come to think of it, there's no really satisfactory definition of a mountain. My dictionary defines it as a 'natural elevation of the earth's surface rising high above surrounding land' but this seems far too vague. Some people think that mountains are hills more than 3,000 feet in height which, if true, would exclude hundreds, possibly thousands, of worthy peaks in Scotland and almost all the fells in Lakeland. Besides, a natural elevation of the earth's surface twice this height in Switzerland might be no more than a cow pasture and, in the Himalayas, the most insignificant foothill. Others would put the qualifying height for mountains as low as 2,000 feet, which would exclude the fine bulk of Black Combe but embrace the relatively insignificant shoulder of Coomb Height at the back of Skiddaw. And then there is the further complication that Scottish mountains are known, colloquially, as hills, and Lakeland peaks as fells. In Scotland Munros are given a special distinction but, in the process, many hills with much more character and shape but falling short of the magic height of 3,000 feet may be considered, by the ignorant, to be of lesser importance and so ignored.

As I explain elsewhere in this book the collection of the Scottish Munros may take even a fairly determined mountaineer most of a lifetime whereas every year dozens of people manage to trot round all the Lake District equivalents in a day. There is, therefore, little challenge in the Lakeland '3,000s' so, setting our sights much lower, we come up with the '2,000s'—the mountains, hills, fells or tops, call them what you will, that make up all the high land in the Lake District. And, right away, you are up against a major snag, for nobody has really decided exactly which are the Lakeland '2,000s' or how many of them there are. Several lists have been made but none exactly agree, for it depends on what rules you apply. Clearly the mountains have to rise above the 2,000 feet contour, but what sort of a dip should there be between one top and the next to merit inclusion? And which maps should be used, since the accuracy of contours varies, and should the summit, for inclusion, have a name or be marked by a spot height or merely indicated by a contour or contours? All these points, and several more, have been studied by the illustrious list-makers, and many anomalies found, so that there is really no firm agreement about how many 2,000-footers there are in the Lake District. Various lists appear from time to time in club journals but these are not readily accessible to the average fell-walker who will probably get more fun out of the game by inventing his own rules about what constitutes a 2,000-feet mountain, compiling a list and then seeing how many of these he has collected in his wanderings. I commend this exercise for a winter's evening, or a succession of winter evenings, when the television's not worth watching or the weather outlook—or the fuel situation—is more than usually depressing.

In the winter of 1973, when the petrol situation and the television news in general seemed as depressing as one could remember, I got out my one-inch Ordnance Survey map and went carefully over every square to see if, after nearly half a century's wanderings over the fells, I had missed any out. It seemed unlikely but, after some time with a magnifying glass, I discovered that to claim to have walked over every single 2,000-feet top in the Lake District, I still had two to do. These are an unnamed height to the west of Haycock and the undistinguished mound, about three miles north-east of Skiddaw House, called Coomb Height which happens to top the 2,000 feet contour by 58 feet. Some day, perhaps, I'll collect them, but I'm in no hurry, for almost all the others were picked up quite incidentally over a lifetime and not with any intention of 'doing the 2,000s'. Indeed, I can only once remember ever going up a Lake District fell because I'd never done it before and that, curiously enough, was Sheffield Pike above Glenridding which I must have skirted scores of times, especially on skiing expeditions. This blatant peak-bagging expedition—for one almost feels obliged to make excuses about this sort of thing, especially in England—was on an autumn day a few years ago and provided some particularly rewarding views of Ullswater. But I remember it mostly for the tea afterwards in a farmhouse kitchen, and especially for the bilberry tart.

To give some idea of the size of this modest undertaking of collecting Lakeland summits, should you wish to get it out of your system, I should explain there are something like 200 tops in the Lake District that exceed 2,000 feet above sea-level. But you could hardly say there are 200 mountains or fells in Lakeland for many of these 'tops' are no more than incidents on a ridge—five, for instance, on Crinkle Crags, four on Birkhouse Moor, and even three on Gray Crag above Pasture Beck in the eastern fells which, when you walk along it, seems almost as level as a roof-tree. All of which serves to underline the persistence and determination of the list-makers while leaving the real value of the exercise somewhat in doubt. To check my own total of tops I used one of the latest of the published lists—that of my friend Francis Falkingham in the journal of the Gritstone Club. He came up with a total of 203 for the Lake District and 349 for the whole of England and he has been single-minded enough to have done the lot. The story of his collection makes interesting reading. He agrees with me that, to put it at its lowest, peak-bagging at least takes you into interesting places, one example of this being his last top—a delightful 2,500 feet rocky summit above Esk Buttress on Scafell Pike which is perhaps only visited by a handful of people in a year compared with the thousands who swarm over the Pike, only half a mile away. Falkingham spent some time on working out a formula for determining which tops should be included, his final definition being any piece of ground with a separate contour ring at 2,000 feet or more on the Ordnance Survey seventh-series, one-inch map. To this he added any points which were obscured on the map by hachuring but which, after visiting and reference to large-scale maps, should clearly be included. This means that some very obscure mounds—such as my missing Coomb Height—are listed, whereas one or two quite distinct little tops, including Helvellyn Low Man which is just over 3,000 feet, are eschewed, which is unfortunate, but if you invent rules you should stick by them. People with magnifying glasses and passions for accuracy may not agree with every one of Falkingham's tops, although I know he checked them all on the ground. For instance, in the Haycock area the map shows Caw Fell at 2,187 feet and an unnamed summit at 2,288 feet, but Falkingham lists Caw Fell at 2,288 feet—I'm sure, correctly—and ignores the other. One snag about the use of a single contour ring is that, at one height, a rise of only 5 feet can produce a ring on the map whereas, at another height, a rise of 45 feet might not do so, which shows how important the ground work must be.

If you walk over every one of Falkingham's 203 tops you could certainly claim to have covered all the high ground of the Lake District over 2,000 feet, but many people, not particularly interested in ticking off every excrescence, may be more interested in knowing how many 2,000-feet mountains or fells there are. To shorten the list you could cut down on the multiple summits like Crinkle Crags, counting just the highest tops in each case, and in this way you will finish up with about 160. But some people may not agree that all these summits are mountains and might quote, for example, Little Gowder Crag which fulfils all the rules for being a top without having much of a claim for being a mountain. Perhaps what most people really want to know, if they are at all interested, is just how many separate mountains there are in the Lake District over 2,000 feet, ignoring tops on a ridge or other irrelevancies, but here again there is ample room for argument. One estimate of these separate mountains is contained in the excellent *Climber and Fellwalker in Lakeland* written by two friends of mine, Frank Monkhouse and Joe Williams. They list 112 of these—a big reduction on my 160 or so—but when you examine their list you find they have left out several tops which some people might well regard as mountain summits. I certainly do not criticize them for this for theirs is clearly stated to be a list of 'peaks'—a word which hardly embraces protuberances or outliers on a major mountain and, indeed, introduces almost a new definition. For, surely, to count as a mountain peak a summit must look something like one, so that the list of Monkhouse and Williams may be somewhere near the heart of the matter. But, even so, they exclude both Broad Crag and Ill Crag in the Scafell range—they happen to be 3,000-feet tops—and also Pillar Rock which is beyond the scope of the average fell-walker anyway, but is much more of a peak than dozens of others included. And they also exclude, oddly enough, Grey Crag above the Shap Fells road which may be an undistinguished summit but is within the National Park, and also Seathwaite Fell, right in the heart of the sanctuary. But these, and I could list others, are merely quibbles. The main facts seem to be that there are about 200 tops in the Lake District above the 2,000 feet contour—although 255 have been discovered by one illustrious researcher—about 160 summits and more than 112 separate mountains, although the exact definition of 'mountain' would have to be agreed by the fussy, and I doubt whether agreement would ever be reached.

Tracking down the 2,000-footers of Lakeland—and, indeed, of England—has kept many highly reputable mountaineers out of mischief for years but plunged them into perhaps more controversy than they had expected. And we still don't really know what a mountain is. But if we take the matter further, above the 2,000 feet contour, we seem to be on surer ground. With some confidence I would say there are 78 tops in the Lake District over 2,500 feet and that, of these, 65 are separate mountains, peaks, fells or whatever you like to call them.

This was the situation in 1973 but it will all be changed when we go metric. We may be proud now of our handful of Lake District 3,000-footers but when mountains are measured in metres instead of feet we will have to eat humble pie for Lakeland will never be able to boast a peak of 1,000 metres. Snowdon will easily be able to step up into this category and Scotland will have scores of 'one-thousanders', but Scafell Pike, the highest mountain in England will have to be content with a prosaic height of 977 metres. And 2,000 feet works out at 610 metres which hasn't much of a ring about it. When mountains are metricated there will only be six of them in the Lake District of more than 900 metres—the new high-level mark of excellence—or nine if you include the tops of Broad Crag, Ill Crag and Helvellyn Low Man. Great End and Bowfell are the two peaks that step into this new top category, which formerly embraced the 3,000-footers, but the graceful mountain of Great Gable, at only 899 metres, will unfortunately be excluded. So, too, will Pillar with only 892 metres. The highest Coniston fells will just make the 800 metres grade but Haycock will miss it by 2 metres. And Pike o' Blisco will make the 'seven hundreds' although Pavey Ark, just across the valley, will fall 3 metres short. Perhaps the 'nine hundreds' will present a new challenge for the record walker for, to include Great End and Bowfell in the day's round of the

Scafells, Helvellyn and Skiddaw, would certainly make a more demanding circuit.

The heights of mountains have always been important to mountaineers but the heights of the Lakeland fells were only fixed with reasonable accuracy about 100 years ago. Before that many of the heights, although surveyed by the instruments of the time, were far from true, and sometimes quite ridiculous. For example, my 1799 edition of Thomas West's *Guide to the Lakes* gives Helvellyn 3,324 feet, which is 211 feet higher than it ought to be, and, even more surprisingly, elevates Cross Fell in the Northern Pennines to the massive height of 3,390 feet and makes it the highest mountain in the Cumbria area. Blencathra—it was called Saddleback in those days—is put among the three-thousanders but the Scafells are not even listed. But the most remarkable conclusion of these eighteenth-century surveyors was that the Yorkshire fells were much higher than those in Lakeland. Ingleborough was given the astonishing height of 3,987 feet—more than 1,600 feet too high—Pen-y-Ghent, 3,930 feet, and Whernside an incredible 4,050 feet—600 feet higher than the height given to Snowdon. And the conclusion from all these observations was that Whernside, which is nowadays regarded as a mere 2,419 feet in height, was 'the highest mountain in South Britain, yet below the point of permanent snow'. At that time Cotopaxi in South America was thought to be the highest mountain in the world at 19,929 feet. Earlier map-makers were even more casual, for my Robert Morden map of Cumberland, dated 1680, shows 'Skiddow Hill', 'Hardknott Hill' and 'Dent Hill' but misses out Helvellyn and the Scafells altogether.

But the Ordnance Survey changed all this rather slipshod surveying and conjecture and, throughout the lifetime of the very oldest of us, have been producing beautiful maps of great accuracy and excellence. We relied on them implicitly and although we might quibble now and again over the shape of a contour, we accepted their mountain heights almost as holy writ. Scafell Pike, the highest mountain in England, was 3,210 feet above sea-level—a particularly easy figure to remember—and we had had it off pat since our schooldays. And then, one day in 1970, some of us woke up to discover that somebody had knocked 4 feet off the Pike, for in the new one-inch tourist map of the Lake District, published by the Ordnance Survey, the mountain was demoted to 3,206 feet. Not only this but Helvellyn was now alleged to be no fewer than 5 feet lower than the 3,118 feet with which it had been credited all my lifetime, while they'd even knocked 2 feet off dear old Coniston Old Man, the highest peak in Lancashire. True, they'd given an extra foot to Skiddaw, Pillar and High Street, but when I got this far in my comparisons I hadn't the heart to pursue the matter further. Anything might have happened; even some of the carefully-counted 2,000-footers might have disappeared. It looked a serious business.

What seemed particularly puzzling was that there was no mention of a new survey on the new map which was based on the same one-inch, seventh-series sheets, but reprinted with the addition of new major roads, some tourist information and such recent additions to the landscape as Wet Sleddale reservoir. I made some local enquiries and was told that since the datum level—or base for the calculation of heights—had been changed from a bench-mark on the dock wall at Liverpool to a rather more picturesque site at Newlyn in Cornwall this could conceivably have had an effect on the heights. But my informant could not account for apparently haphazard changes, some up, some down, some unaltered. A new level, it seemed to me, could only alter the heights in one direction—if it altered them at all. In the course of my enquiries I was given a strangely bizarre explanation by one man with some knowledge of map-making. He thought it was just possible that the new heights might have something to do with 'the shifting of land masses'. Trying to put this in simple terms that I could understand, he explained that where there were increasing pressures anywhere on the globe there had to be corresponding increases and decreases in height all over the place. 'Indeed,' he confided, 'the land may well be going down in the south of England and rising up in the north—a sort of tilting motion,' but this fearsome possibility was more than I could swallow and, in any case, didn't seem to have much to do with Scafell Pike losing 4 feet and Skiddaw gaining one.

But, eventually, the Ordnance Survey headquarters in Southampton were good enough to provide me with a full explanation of the changes and readers may find this illuminating. The revised heights, they explained, were derived from recent re-observation and computation of their triangulation network and in some cases differed from the old heights which had been based on observations made about 100 years before. Where there was a triangulation pillar at or near the summit of a mountain the height on the map usually referred, they said, to ground level at the pillar and they believed these heights to be accurate to plus or minus one foot in terms of absolute altitude above their national levelling datum at Newlyn in Cornwall. The old heights had been based on spirit levelling from Liverpool, used before 1921 as the national datum, whereas the new values were based on modern instruments and techniques and were believed to be more reliable. The Ordnance Survey went on to explain further that, on the majority of mountains, the triangulation pillar is placed on the highest point. Apparently, the new heights for Skiddaw, Pillar and High Street refer to such points and the differences I had noted were due to the new and more accurate values having been used. However, where the triangulation station was not on the highest point of the mountain, which is apparently the situation on Scafell Pike, Helvellyn, and Coniston Old Man—although I must say I had not noticed this—the Ordnance Survey had had to decide whether to show the height of the triangulation pillar or the height at the top of the mountain. There was often insufficient space on one-inch maps to show both heights clearly. Each case, they said, was carefully considered on its merits and for these three mountains they had decided to show ground-level height at the triangulation station, since this referred to a specifically identifiable mark. But when the larger-scale maps were revised and published it would generally be possible to show both heights in such cases.

The Ordnance Survey also dealt with the height of Ben Macdhui, the second highest mountain in Britain. The most recently computed value of natural ground level below the pillar and cairn compared reasonably well, they said, with the old value of 4,298 feet which was therefore being retained on maps. The height of 4,300 feet, which had appeared on the Cairngorms tourist map and on one of the one-inch sheets, referred to the height of the top of the cairn. This height would be revised as new editions appeared and, meanwhile, the height of 4,296 feet was shown on the latest editions of the one-inch sheet and the Cairngorms tourist map.

In general, the Ordnance Survey say, very properly, that it is impracticable to revise and reprint every map every time new data becomes available. Many height changes, they say, have appeared over the past few years but it was only when mountains with famous names were involved that the practice became apparent. Mountaineers will appreciate this and agree with me that we all owe an immense debt to the Ordnance Survey for their painstakingly accurate work over so many years. Mountain maps, to most of us, are things of beauty, recalling many long days in the hills, and a most essential part of our equipment.

I notice that the latest Lake District tourist map not only altered the heights of some of the principal mountains but also changed some of the spot heights and the heights of the lower fells, such as Gowbarrow Fell. Many new roads were also shown, a great deal of tourist information and, for the first time, Robinson's Cairn near Pillar Rock—demolished by vandals two or three years later and then rebuilt by voluntary wardens. Another completely new development on the map was the delineation of what were described as 'viewpoints'. These took us back about 200 years to the very first of the guide-book writers, Father Thomas West, the gentle Jesuit. In his splendidly inaccurate guide, first published in 1778, Father West laid down a number of 'stations' from which the best views in Lakeland—in his opinion—could be obtained. He listed these in order of importance and suggested they should be viewed through 'landscape mirrors' of plano-convex glass. You stood with your back to the view and looked at the scenery through the mirror, 'which removes objects to a due distance and shows them in the soft colours of nature'. From the new Ordnance Survey viewpoints, however, you are presumably supposed to look out at the view and not turn your back on it.

The one-inch Ordnance Survey map remains the best all-purpose map for the walker and mountaineer, although it is sometimes criticized for containing too much information which may tend to be confusing. Larger-scale maps are more accurate so far as contours and special features are concerned, but the fell-walker may have to use several on one walk. During recent years specialist maps for the climber have appeared, which clearly indicate all the crags but exclude a great deal of other information that could have been useful. On occasions I have used the former two-and-a-half-inch map, but most of my maps for nearly every mountain district in Britain—a whole shelf full of them—are one-inch maps and they have never let me down, although I have found minor inaccuracies, here and there. Maps are perhaps the best reminder of mountain days for with them you can retrace your wanderings and recall experiences—especially when their bedraggled condition reminds you of stormy days on the tops. On long, difficult walks in winter or in mist I sometimes work out the compass bearings in advance—often a trying operation during bad weather in the mountains—and these bearings on the side of the map also remind me of these days. Every time I go into a new mountain area, either in Britain or abroad, I buy the relevant maps and a glance at these tells their own story. My most tattered maps are those of the north-west Highlands which recall a fortnight of incessant rain, but other maps, including those for Ullapool and the Glen Affric country, still look new, suggesting good weather, with the tops clear of mist. My Lake District maps are numerous and varied, the most bedraggled being tattered and torn and barely readable. One lives permanently in a rucksack pocket. Some of them show my own tiny contribution to the accuracy of the Ordnance Survey—the replacement of the former Earnest Crag in Deepdale by the proper name of Ern Nest Crag, which the Ordnance Survey changed at my instigation after they had carefully examined my arguments. Ever since I came upon a handful of surveyors building a triangulation column in bad weather in the High Street fells about forty years ago I have had an affection and respect for the men of the Ordnance Survey who have contributed so much to our knowledge of the mountains. Without maps many of our mountain wanderings would be aimless and unsatisfying, and in unfamiliar country we might achieve very little. But although I have such a high regard for the painstaking accuracy of the Ordnance Survey I am tempted to have just one friendly dig at them. In their 1970 revision of the tourist map of the Lake District they allowed the colour picture of Ashness Bridge on the cover to be printed the wrong way round.

A REAL ROCK GARDEN

On a breezy afternoon of showers and sunshine with becks in lively spate I suddenly came upon the biggest natural rock garden I have ever seen. It stretches for hundreds of yards along the true right wall of the tremendous ravine of Black Force which dramatically cleaves the rounded Howgills at the side of the former county boundary of Carlin Gill. Black Force, which looks across the long, dog-legged gill, is one of the most exciting bits of scenery for miles—the more so because all around are smooth, gentle fells that you could almost walk in your sleep. But you need your eyes open and some agility to get up or down Black Force, particularly when the waterfalls are crashing down the rocks, and once inside the ravine you can easily imagine yourself in some wild corner of the Hindu Kush instead of 2 or 3 miles from the motorway and the main line to Euston. The rock garden is precipitous, several hundred feet high and best seen from the opposite side of the ravine, when lit by sunshine after rain. Hanging over the leaping waters are rowans with here and there a stunted birch, and, massed above and among them, are scores of clumps of purple heather, green and yellowing ferns, great beds of blaeberry, banks of thyme, shy saxifrages and, woven between, a colourful carpet of mountain flowers. Sparkling in the sunlight the dripping rocks neatly separate the splashes of colour with overhangs, ledges and walls so that you could have sworn that a landscape gardener had been at work, but nobody has ever used hammer or trowel on this wall apart from Nature herself. And the pools below the garden could only have been built in Paradise.

10

Tackling the Munros

A Progress Report on a Long Job

It should be firmly stated, right from the start, that I have not done the Munros—the 3,000-feet mountains of Scotland. For years I have been quietly ticking them off—almost ashamedly, for Munro-bagging is the sort of thing that respectable mountaineers usually keep to themselves—but I still have some way to go. Very shortly though, when I may be able to spend more time in the hills, I hope to be granted sufficient energy to complete my list, for the leisurely collection of summits seems a proper occupation for a mountaineer who is beginning to find steep rock intimidating but still enjoys reasonably good health. But, although ticking off remote Scottish mountains just because they happen to attain a certain height may sound almost indecent to some mountaineers, it does at least give you the incentive to explore parts of the country well removed from the Highlands of the motor-car tourist. And readers may be prepared to accept some scattered memories of long days in the heather or in remote, untracked corries, although I have yet to reach many summits that rear above the magic 3,000 feet contour.

Munro-bagging is a disease that afflicts the middle-aged and elderly. If infected earlier in life, you tend to be diverted away from much more worth-while adventures such as hard rock-climbing, demanding winter ascents, alpine experience, exploration and so on, and become a mere peak-bagger, unable to see the mountain for the contours. And by yielding too soon to the insidious attraction of Munro's tables you are liable to miss out altogether many of the most rewarding mountains in Scotland, for Munros, although the highest, are by no means necessarily the best mountains. Several of them, indeed, are quite boring. The middle-aged or elderly mountaineer, however, who decides to embark on this slightly strange mission is likely to have enjoyed these lesser, but much more splendid, peaks in the days when he was a free man of the hills and not just an old-fashioned walker bemused and swaddled by contour lines. But don't leave your Munro-bagging too late. A doctor friend of mine, a good walker and climber, told me that he intended to get down seriously to the Munros when he retired at 60. He was then 59 and when I asked him how many he had done he replied: 'One, Ben Nevis.' He is now working through the list, steadily but slowly, and I wish him well, but already he confesses he did not realize the size of the problem. For there are a lot of Munros, and for most people, unless they live in the Highlands and have plenty of spare time, the task takes many years and, sometimes, most of a lifetime.

Munros were invented by a Victorian and their collection later became the Holy Grail of determined Edwardian mountaineers in Norfolk jackets. The tables were originally compiled by Hugh Munro (later Sir Hugh T. Munro, Bt., of Lindertis, Kirriemuir, in the county of Forfar) in 1891 and first published in the journal of the Scottish Mountaineering Club of which Munro was at one time the president. Munro, who was a great walker, had the idea of climbing all the Scottish mountains of 3,000 feet or more but died in 1919 when he still had two to do—one of them in the Cairngorms and the other the Inaccessible Pinnacle in Skye. His original tables listed 538 'tops' of 3,000 feet or upwards, of which he considered 283 to be separate mountains, but these totals have been revised from time to time, the latest figures being 277 separate mountains and 545 'tops'. Over the years the separate mountains have come to be known as 'Munros' and the subsidiary summits as 'Munro tops', so that the peak-bagger has two targets at which to aim—the collection of the 277 Munros or the more formidable task of including all the tops as well. The first man to climb all the Munros—283 were listed in those days—was the Revd. A. E. Robertson who completed the job in 1901 and another Scotsman, R. Burn, was the first mountaineer, in 1923, to include all the tops as well, the total in those days being 558. J. Rooke Corbett was the first Englishman to do all the Munros and the subsidiary tops while J. A. Parker, after climbing all the Munros, went on to become the first man to climb all the 3,000-feet mountains in the British Isles. Mrs John Hirst had the distinction of being the first woman to complete all the mountains and the tops in Munro's tables—with her husband as companion.

Many friends of mine, with either more time or more determination than myself, have done all the Munros, and several of them the subsidiary tops as well. One of them who believes he was about the twelfth man to complete all the Munros and the tops, in 1960, tells me he had climbed between 75 and 100 of them before he had even heard of Munros. He estimates that probably between 80 and 100 people have now completed the larger task and I believe that at least one man has climbed all the Munros twice. One of the first Englishmen to complete the Munros and the tops was Colin Dodgson of Grasmere and he did most of them in the winter months—the only time he could get away from running his tourists' cafe. And his companion on most of the peaks, including all the Munros, was the village shoemaker at Grasmere, Timothy Tyson, who was nearly 70 years of age when they climbed their last Munro—Ben More on the island of Mull. Not content with this, and many other achievements, the pair then got down to the more original task of bathing in every tarn in the Lake District and they finished these off—463 of them—when Tim was in his seventy-sixth year.

People not so familiar with maps as Munro-baggers have to be, may be surprised to read that the totals of 3,000-feet mountains in Scotland may change from time to time, as if, every now and again, new mountains are mysteriously emerging. The explanation is, of course, that when you start counting mountains you have to decide exactly what a mountain is, and it is surprisingly difficult to get agreement about this. Contours show you, clearly enough, the ground above 3,000 feet, and there's a great deal of this in Scotland, but you've got to decide, in all this high land, what constitutes a mountain, a subsidiary top or merely an incident on a ridge. Nowadays, it is generally agreed that a Munro is a separate mountain with a drop of at least 500 feet between it and the next peak or separated from it by a long distance or some particular climbing difficulty. Munro tops are more difficult to determine, but the editor of the 1953 edition of the tables suggested that there should be a dip of at least 75 to 100 feet of decided gradient to the col separating it from another top, and that the mountain should also have 'some kind of individuality', marking it off as a distinct portion of the ridge and not a mere undulation. To quote an English example, there are seven summits in the Lake District exceeding 3,000 feet in height, but if these were in Scotland only three of them—Scafell Pike, Helvellyn and Skiddaw—would certainly count as Munros, Scafell being doubtful and Broad Crag, Ill Crag and Helvellyn Low Man clearly being no more than tops at the best, and probably not even that. Beinn Tarsuinn was only included in the Munro tables in 1953, after the compilers had concluded that the map of the area was very casual, due, it was thought, to bad weather and also to the fact that the surveyors 'had been hurried in order to meet the views of the then laird'. Ordnance Survey maps, indeed, are constantly revised with mountain names often altered and heights increased or decreased by a few feet. In recent years there have been many changes in height and I refer to some Lake District changes elsewhere in this book. One recently reported change of height was gratefully received by mountaineers—including myself when I last went up Aonach Mor in Lochabar, the eighth highest Munro in Scotland. The table gives the mountain 3,999 feet but I am told that it is now 4,000 feet, so that there are now thirteen tops in Scotland of 4,000 feet or higher. But there will always be arguments about Munros and tops and all the ordinary peakbagger can do is to tick them off in the tables and hope that, while he is doing this, nobody will slip in any more. Metrication, which will produce about 250 tops of 1,000 metres or higher in Scotland—but not one in England—may be a further complication.

But looking back on forty years of mountaineering in Scotland, including the ascent of many fine hills that do not qualify as Munros, my thoughts are not on totals, heights and contour lines but rather on the size and rich variety of all this mountain splendour that lies so conveniently near to those of us fortunate enough to live in the north of England. I have often stood on an alpine peak and been thrilled by the sight of hundreds of mountains stretching, all round the compass, to the horizon, but you can see much the same sight in Scotland, especially in winter-time. The Scottish hills, of course, are very much smaller, but the general impression is much the same—mountains everywhere, as far as the eye can see, in blue or white ripples, reaching to the farthest sky and, sometimes, across the sea. Somewhere between the ridges are valleys, roads, towns and people but you don't see them—just the encircling hills and, perhaps, below

Approaching Thornthwaite Crag

Blea Water and Harter Fell

The Howgills from Firbank Fell

your feet, the nearest lochans. Nobody—or, at best, a handful of people—knows how many mountains there are in Scotland. We have counted the Munros but there are many thousands of mountains—or hills, as they call even the biggest in Scotland—and you could hide the whole of the Lake District in one corner. And just to climb the best of them can be a lifetime's task for most people—hundreds of splendid days in remote, untracked country known only to a few shepherds and gillies, the red deer and the eagles. I have often walked all day in these hills and not seen another human being or even a track or cairn, let alone orange peel and empty beer cans. Nowadays I can reach Scotland, if I drive hard, in one hour from my house and I sometimes regret that I did not make many more visits in the days before the tourist invasion that has spoiled so many delectable places. But I am more fortunate than most in living so close to this wonderful mountain country and having had the chance to start my Scottish mountain exploration in the early 1930s.

My first Munros were picked up in Skye but it was not until after the Second World War that I bought my copy of Munro's tables and started to tick off those I had done. There were, I remember, more than fifty of them, but the widely separated ticks only served to show the size of the task remaining—if I decided to tackle it. At first it was a very casual business indeed and it was only in advanced middle-age that I started anything approaching a serious onslaught. As a rock-climber I knew the crags before I knew the mountains and the first Munros were only picked up incidentally as part of climbing days. The first on the mainland were, therefore, peaks like Ben Nevis, Buachaille Etive More and Bidean nam Bian and, being an early skier in the days before mountain roads and chair-lifts, the Cairngorm summits were also familiar before the war. Scottish mountains, besides being high, are often very remote, at the head of lonely glens far from habitation, so that they cannot all be collected by leisurely assaults from comfortable hotels. It is necessary to camp to bag some of them and many enthusiasts, although not myself, have bivouacked in the heather to add outlying summits to their list. Like most people who have spent some time in the Scottish hills I have used every type of accommodation including tents, huts, caravans, youth hostels, bed and breakfast places, farmhouses, shooting lodges and hotels, good and bad. I have slept in motor cars, caravettes and bothies more comfortably than in some hotels, and the youth hostels used have included some of the most primitive and a particularly sumptuous one, at Garth near Loch Tay, where the facilities included a quiet room with a Steinway grand. One of the most interesting youth hostels was at Inver Alligin in Torridon—regrettably closed down many years ago—where we first entered to see wet socks hanging over soup simmering on a blackened stove and a bearded man sitting on the floor in the semi-darkness frying fish on a primus. There was no fuel but we managed to dig earthy bits of coal out of the ground where the heap had been, and the entrance to the women's dormitory, I seem to remember, was a rickety ladder. The place seemed little better than a howff but we had one of our best holidays from this base where the atmosphere, apart from being dark and fuggy, was remarkably friendly and jolly and the company of the very best.

This visit to the Highlands more than twenty years ago—we stayed in several youth hostels that year, having a young family—happened to coincide with the wettest fortnight of the year, which, at one stroke, eliminated two of the major snags about holidaying in Scotland in August—the incessant rain or, at best, a clammy Scotch mist, the midges and the deer-stalkers crawling over many of the best mountains. All we had to endure, this time, was rain which washed away the midges and ensured that the deer-shooters were trapped in their lodges, unable to stir. The previous few weeks had been extremely hot, with the midges operating in record numbers, and it was reported in the daily press that workmen on the Garve road had downed tools and gone home because somebody had forgotten the 'Dimp'. The rain began as soon as we headed north and, although no doubt millions of midges were waiting in the heather to beset us as soon as it stopped, it continued to rain incessantly for the fortnight and we were spared their attacks. On the way north we did a training walk over Carn Mor Dearg and Ben Nevis and although we picked up four tops considerably higher than Scafell Pike, we never saw any of them. This was our first wetting, right through to the skin, but before the end of the holiday we had got used to it. On the way up to the Ben from the Arête we bumped into a man coming down who said he had spent ten minutes on top trying to find the observatory but had failed to do so.

An interesting feature of this holiday, which demanded careful navigation work every day, was our compass. Having lost my own earlier in the year I was, I suppose, extremely fortunate to find one, a few weeks later, lying at the top of Walker's Gully on Pillar Rock. As it would not work I presented it to my son Robin, who was about 13 years of age, and then, stupidly, forgot to buy a compass on the way through Glasgow and found I could not get one in Fort William. There was no mountain shop there in those days. In the meantime Robin had dropped the compass several times and this must have done the trick for, when we suddenly remembered it before our first walk, we found it had started working again. It only really failed us once and that was on the top of Liathach. It was the usual kind of day, pouring with rain and a little sleet as well, with the cloud down to 500 feet all day. In those days the road to Torridon was not unlike the bottom of a river bed, a fact I clearly remember because I had foolishly agreed to drive a motorcycle halfway along the road to Kinlochewe for the bearded man first encountered frying fish in the hostel. He was going to traverse Liathach from west to east and then pick up his motorbike, whereas we, with my car at the other end, were going to do the walk in the opposite direction. It was many years since I had last driven a motorcycle and I do not intend to repeat the experience—not, at least, on such difficult terrain.

By steering a course straight up the screes and through the cloud, we managed to find the first summit and then, trusting to our battered Walker's Gully compass, made our way along the whole ridge with its several tops, including the Fasarinen Pinnacles, although never seeing more than a few feet ahead. But at the far end of the ridge, where it broadens out, the compass suddenly became temperamental and we were alarmed to find that by turning it round we could get the needle to point in any direction we wished. There was only one thing to do, the time-honoured device of keeping the wind on the same cheek, with the result that we made a completely unpremeditated descent of the north slopes of Sgorr a' Chadail, landing miles up the then trackless Coire Mhic Nobuil, with the river in violent spate, instead of in Torridon. The journey back to the hostel, drenched through to the skin and boots filled through wading burns knee-deep, was tiring and I sent Robin on to Inver Alligin while I walked the several miles round the mountain to pick up the car. Squelching along the road, unable to smoke since my matches were as limp as wet macaroni, I met the Torridon postman. 'Good evening' he said, 'nice drop of rain,' but I hadn't the strength to argue with him.

We reserved, however, the wettest day for An Teallach. The night before, I rang up the baronet who owned the mountain and asked him whether he would be shooting deer the following day. He replied that that was his intention but added that An Teallach was quite impossible and dangerous in bad weather. Would I telephone him the next morning to check? The telephone was only 50 yards away from what was then the Dundonnell youth hostel where we were staying but when I reached it after breakfast the following day I was already wet through. It was, in other words, a perfect non-shooting day and Sir Michael Peto was able to tell me that the deer-stalking was off. He suggested that we should return the following May to do An Teallach but when he realized our determination to get up the mountain, no matter what the weather, he proved extremely pleasant and co-operative. He recited a list of people who had come to grief on the mountain in bad weather, suggested a route well away from his deer, asked us to do as little shouting and banging as possible, and finally gave us his blessing.

The day proved quite remarkable and I doubt whether I have ever seen the hills so wet. We traversed the ridge, although missing out the outlying summits, but never saw anything except the few yards of rocky pinnacles ahead for the thick cloud cut off the yawning depths below. On the descent we never even saw Loch Toll an Lochain, the celebrated viewpoint, although we stood on its shores. The water was running an inch deep off the slabs in the corries and we were over our boot-tops at nearly every step. On the lower slopes when we emerged from the worst of the cloud we saw ptarmigan and then, very low down, about fifty of Sir Michael's deer but, as requested, we passed them without a sound, save that from our squelching boots.

We were not ticking off Munros that fortnight but climbing mountains that looked interesting, a procedure to be commended to all except those who, by reason of age or infirmity, want to get the Munros out of their system before it is too late. For this reason we did several mountains of less than 3,000 feet—peaks despised, or at least neglected, by the most single-minded Munro fanatics but, despite this, among the best mountains in Scotland. An Stac (popularly, Stack Polly) went easily in a morning. This was long before the days of the car-park at its foot, the eroded tracks to the summit col, and the specially constructed tourist route to the ridge. We simply took a compass bearing from what seemed the foot of the mountain and slogged up through the thick mist and pouring rain. The occasional view of a spike of rock along the summit ridge from its adjacent spike was quite interesting, but that was all we saw. It was good to note how well vibram soles stick on Torridon sandstone when the water is streaming over your toecap. Suilven proved a particularly hard day. We made the mistake of calling at Glen Canisp Lodge, braving the warning notices about the danger of stray bullets, to ask permission to go into the deer forest and were directed to a keeper's cottage. Here we had to swallow our pride and ask the occupants in which direction our mountain lay for, although Suilven is the most prominent feature of the countryside for many miles around, we had not seen it all week and the mist, as usual, was more or less down to the deck. We noted the direction on our invaluable compass and followed this line for what seemed several hours, but must have been shorter. We never saw the vestige of a track, and there was never a distant aiming-point on which to set the compass. The situation was further complicated by the fact that every time we ascended one of the innumerable hillocks that bestrew this area we found we were separated from the next by a depressing-looking lochan that had to be circumnavigated on a different compass bearing. It was, needless to say, pouring with rain, the going was appalling, and we didn't seem to be getting anywhere, when quite suddenly we more or less walked slap into Caisteal Liath (the Grey Castle), and knew that the day would eventually be ours. We managed to find our way round to the north of the mountain and, when we thought we had gone far enough, crawled up the steep heather and scree to the summit ridge. It was then an easy matter to turn sharp right, squelch up to the highest point and enjoy the experience, for a few drenching seconds, of standing on the summit of the mountain that some people declare is the best viewpoint in Scotland. But all I could see was my very wet son, in my second-best anorak, standing about 3 feet away, with the rain streaming down his face and bubbling out of his boots.

There was, of course, one consolation for all this bog-trotting—a most rewarding day. The torrential rain one morning, following about ten other similarly wet mornings, must have affected our moral fibre for we did not set off until about 2.30 p.m. in a heavy downpour and thick mist, to deal with the Ben More Coigach group. The compass got us to the top of Beinn nan Caorach and we were plotting the direction to the next top when, almost miraculously, the rain stopped and the clouds began to lift. We pushed on with all speed, fearing the mist would come down again, but, as if to reward us for all those wet days in the clouds, the sun came out—the only time we saw it on the mountains during the holiday—and we reached the top of Sgurr an Fhidleir in the most perfect weather. From this remarkable summit, from which drops a 700-feet high precipice, we saw An Stac and, beyond it, Suilven—peaks we had climbed but never seen. And, beyond that again, we saw some of the most northerly mountains on the Scottish mainland and, in between, scores of lochans glistening in the sunshine, and a wild, lovely countryside. With our wet clothes steaming in the sunshine we hurried on to the top of Ben More Coigach itself and then along the rocky ridge to the last peak overlooking the sea.

And this was the view that made the whole holiday worth while. Far below, sparkling in the evening sun and so close we felt we could have dropped a stone into the depths, was the deep, blue sea, the waves breaking white on a dozen yellow beaches fringed with grey-brown rocks, and the sea-birds wheeling and screaming over the tide. Just off the coast, like great ships at anchor, lay the Summer Isles, while beyond the sea we could see the magic outer islands and, far to the south, rose the dark spires of An Teallach. We trod down the heather with the smell of the peat from the crofters' fires in our nostrils, the whirr of a million insects in the undergrowth in our ears, the sight of the sunset over the Atlantic to enjoy, and the thoughts of a good dinner to keep us going.

I have returned many times to these wonderful northern Highlands since this wet fortnight and reclimbed the mountains we had trodden but not seen. An Teallach in fine weather is one of the most splendid mountains in Scotland with ten tops over 3,000 feet but only counting as one Munro. Similarly, Liathach is only one Munro although it has six summits, five of them over 3,000 feet, so that both of them are particularly rewarding peaks for the ticker-off of tops but hard work, if you do the whole mountain, for the seeker after Munros. Our second An Teallach visit could hardly have been more different from the first—sunny skies, with views across half of Scotland, and hardly a breath of wind. We were camping that year and had arranged to meet friends from Cumberland for some hill-walking. When they saw our tent, on the edge of a burn tumbling down to the main road from the lower slopes of the hill—the site has now been swallowed up by new road works in recent years—they said they had rarely seen such a stupid site, and pitched their tent near the roadside about half a mile away. But we had our revenge the following morning for there was a thunderstorm during the night which flooded out their tent and left ours, pitched on a tiny knoll, completely unaffected. This strategic victory seemed to have an effect on our morale for, while the others were content with traversing the main ridge of the mountain, Robin and I did all ten tops—a useful day's contribution if you have the Munro tops in mind. At the end of the day we slithered down a scree gully to the loch—seen properly for the first time—and trotted down a thyme-scented hillside to a fried Angus steak by the shore of Little Loch Broom.

Looking through old diaries, 1957 seems to have been a good Scottish year for me. There was an early visit to the Merrick country in the Galloway hills, a June holiday in the mountains of Argyll, and a concentrated attack on the Munros in August. Galloway has no interest for the Munro-bagger for although The Merrick is the highest Scottish mountain south of the Highlands it only reaches 2,764 feet. But this is just another example of how much of the best of Scotland is missed if you concentrate merely on the 3,000-footers. Here in Galloway are nearly thirty mountains over 2,000 feet in height, at least fifty lochans, great crags and waterfalls, lovely trout and salmon rivers, a romantic history and some of the most inaccessible farms and cottages in the country. If you want to be alone in the mountains the trackless Galloway hills may well suit you, and the very names have a romantic ring about them—names like Nick of the Dungeon, Backhill of the Bush, Black Water of Dee, Rig of the Jarkness, Spout of the Clints, Door of the Cairnsmore, the Hags of Borgan, and so on. One place, close to the Deil's Dyke and the Grey Mare's Tail, is called briefly The Thieves and, not far away, there is the Castle of Old Risk. One day I arranged to cross the mountains and meet a friend who was to spend the time, in a distant valley, fishing for supper. My one encounter of the day, I remember, was with four fine red deer that had trotted up through the corrie to a gap in the ridge, delightfully known as the Nick of the Curleywee. I was seated above the gap on a rock ledge having my lunch and was able to watch the deer, no more than 50 yards away, for about five minutes. Three of them had massive antlered heads and the fourth was a youngster, only half their size. They saw me but, as I made no movement and the wind was blowing across their line of vision, they stood their ground, turning every now and again as if to show off their magnificent antlers. Ten minutes after they had decided to trot down into the next valley a very tiny fawn, not much bigger than a dog, climbed slowly up to the gap—perhaps the others had been waiting for it—but it panicked when it saw me and tumbled, helter-skelter, down the rough mountainside.

Over the years I have seen red deer in the mountains on scores of occasions, including a herd of 200 in the Arran hills and once, down in the Mar Forest near Braemar in winter, a herd of up to 1,000, grazing like cattle just below the snowline. My latest encounter was in the Aonachs, north of Ben Nevis, in the autumn of 1973 when I almost stumbled on a great red stag with two hinds—the only living creatures I had seen all day. I was so close, perhaps the length of a cricket pitch away, that I could almost see the beast's reflexes working, as he sized up the situation and then, throwing out his great chest, bounded down the hillside with his followers in pursuit.

For the 1957 visit to Argyll we had a sun-drenched week—up to 80 degrees in the shade and even higher the day we went up Ben Cruachan. The hottest day in Glasgow for many years, reported the newspapers. But we were able to kick steps in old, hard snow up to the summit and, a day or two later, on Bidean nan Bian, the highest mountain in Argyll, there were drifts several hundred yards long with the snow frozen solid in places. It was so hot on Ben Cruachan that I set fire to the mountain by mistake. I had found the skull and antlers of a red deer and was trying to take a colour photograph of the distant island of Mull, framed by the antlers on the bare hillside, when I smelled burning. Looking round, I saw a square yard of grass and heather that I had just traversed well ablaze and can only assume that the fire had been caused by a speck of ash from my pipe. It was the work of a few moments to kick it out but it emphasized to me the difficulties of the Forestry Commission in their rapidly growing Scottish forests in summer-time. Another memory of that day is of reaching the car, parked on the Pass of Brander, to find that the seats were too hot to sit on. It was an open car and had been parked full in the blazing sun all day. We had to sit on our anoraks to drive down to the pub at Taynuilt and persuade them—it was a Sunday and they had a six-day licence then—that, having been over the Ben Cruachan peaks, we were indeed bona fide travellers.

Winter in Scotland

The lower slopes of Ben Nevis

The An Teallach ridge

The Ben Nevis cliffs

The Loch Cluanie hills

Beinn Eighe

This was a Scottish holiday with memories of velvety pink and purple cushions of moss campion growing in rock crevices just below some of the finest summits in Britain, of evening dips into deep, dark pools among the pine trees, of the smell of wood-smoke and tangle along a loch shore within sight of the Cuillin of Skye, of early morning sunlight on the great rock buttresses of Bidean, and of the westering sun setting behind the blue hills of Morven, beyond Tobermory, beyond Ardnamurchan and the farthest tip of the Scottish mainland, beyond the Outer Islands and the sea.

Later that same year my boy and I went over the summits of the Five Sisters of Kintail which look down on the road through Glen Shiel on the way to Skye. Actually we went over seven summits, not five, four of them over 3,000 feet with considerable gaps in between, but our total of Munros for the day was only two. During that August holiday we ascended fourteen mountains over 3,000 feet but collected only seven Munros for our pains. We scrambled along the Aonach Eagach ridge, that splendid walk high above Glencoe that makes such a magnificent expedition in winter, finishing up with a very quick, zigzag trot without a pause, all the way down to the Clachaig Inn, which suggests that we must have been very fit or very thirsty. Part of the time we spent in Glen Affric, Glen Cannich and Strath Farrar, among the longest and most beautiful valleys in Scotland but comparatively little visited, for they are not only remote but restricted due to hydro-electric operations. We discovered a gate across the track in Strath Farrer, could only reach the dam in Glen Cannich on wheels, and found a private road, with no cars allowed, in Glen Affric. The difficulties were overcome in different ways, generally involving a great deal of hard work, but permission was gained in Glen Affric to drive along the private road to the lodge when the keeper, a sympathetic soul, learned that we wanted to walk over Mam Soul and Carn Eige, the twelfth and thirteenth highest Munros in Scotland. This was quite an active holiday but I can still remember the more leisurely moments—the distant views of Skye and the Outer Isles from craggy mainland peaks, the unspoiled perfection of tiny seashore villages like Plockton and Glenelg, wonderful summer evenings drifting in a boat on Loch Duich and planning what to brew up for supper, the sweet scent of the thyme among the heather, and Scottish country dancing in a lamp-lit room to the wild skirling of the pipes.

There were other years when the children were younger and a walk to Lochnagar from the youth hostel in Glen Clova was considered too much of an expedition for the boy, so that Tom Price and I left him behind. We picked up several tops besides Lochnagar that day of crisp snow and warm sunshine—and Robin and I later added a few more—but the principal memory of that visit was an early morning encounter with an owl. Tom was sleeping in his motor car and making meals over fires made from damp wood in all sorts of strange places, but one night I persuaded him to try out the luxury of youth hostel life. During supper we were introduced to the owl, regarded as a resident, and fed him with bacon scraps, but early the following morning Tom awoke me from an adjoining bunk in the dormitory and asked me to have a look at the foot of my bed. There I saw the owl looking at me with what appeared some ferocity and we were both so alarmed that we decided we must persuade him to leave so that we could go back to sleep. The next half-hour was exasperating, exciting and somewhat dangerous but, somehow or another, we managed to get him out of the window. But that was the end of youth hostels for Tom; thereafter he preferred the comparative safety of his motor car bedroom.

I think it was on this holiday that we made a mass family attack on the Ben Lawers range. Our daughter, Sandra, was very young but we managed to get her up the main peak, largely by persuading her on repeated occasions that the snow patches a little higher up the mountain would be admirable for sliding down on her anorak—an entertainment she had recently discovered. In this way, with many pauses and many sliding demonstrations ourselves, which meant that we had to ascend much of the mountain twice, we gradually, bit by bit, got her to the top, after which the mountaineers went on to traverse other tops in the range.

One year I had the good fortune to run into a Munro-bagging party and be invited to accompany them in an assault on the hills north of Loch Cluanie, well east of the Five Sisters of Kintail. The party included old friends Neil and Jill Mather, and a remarkably sprightly retired surgeon, Jimmy Dawson, who were camping at Shiel Bridge. It was a bright, clear morning with the promise of superb long-distance views, but it was not long before I realized that these were people who didn't believe in wasting too much time in looking at scenery. The pace was set by a young man just back from the Alps and in superb condition and Neil was in training for the Lake District Mountain Trial; the rest of us just had to keep up. We went up the first top, Carn Ghluasaid, without a stop, as if we were competing in the Grasmere guides' race—Jimmy and I stripped to the waist—and continued, in much the same fashion, over six more tops, until somebody—probably me—suggested that perhaps we might start the walk back. Jimmy had to be dissuaded from collecting several more tops—I remember his pointing longingly to distant ranges, not individual peaks, and suggesting that they should be included—but eventually we turned round and began to work our way back towards the main glen. On one occasion we paused to look at some deer grazing in the corries far below but, quite clearly, dawdling was not allowed and we ran all the way down to the glen from the last peak in a lather of sweat. Two of us seized the opportunity on the way down for a quick dip in a rock pool—one of the quickest bathes I have ever had, in and out and no time for towelling, even if we had had any—and we reached the Cluanie Inn in exactly the right state for several quick pints. This was a most rewarding day, snatched out of a rather more leisurely week with my wife who had gone off to look at waterfalls. We had collected a fair haul of Munro tops but Neil still had enough energy left to go for a training run that evening. He needed the exercise, he said.

Much of my mountain walking in Scotland, particularly during the last five or six years, has been alone—a practice which has suited me well enough although not to be recommended to all and sundry. I enjoy the company of friends in the hills but this cannot always be arranged in often hastily-planned family holidays, and the freedom of lone walking has many attractions. With the children now grown-up and, in one case, several thousand miles away, Scottish holidays for some years now have often been taken with my wife as sole companion and she is not so single-minded about high hills as myself. Our practice, therefore, is often to set off together up some long glen and then for me to leave her to continue a leisurely walk to a pass, bothy or waterfall while I scurry off to the tops. Timings are so worked out that she normally arrives back at the car in just the right time to have a welcome brew of tea ready for me at the end of my round of the mountains. This may sound selfish, and probably is, but at least my wife has had an interesting day, without having to go at my speed, and each of us has seen a great deal missed by the other. One day in the Grey Corries my wife fell in with a party of deer-stalkers and was able to watch the whole operation, right up to the time when they dragged the stag by its antlers down the hill and on to the waiting pony. The weather for her that day was fine and sunny while I was in the clouds in a hailstorm. Over the years we have so perfected this selfish system that I am normally observed returning when still a mile or so away, so that the tea is just brewed when I arrive. I particularly remember one beautifully timed arrival to a woodside alfresco meal after a long hot day on the Beinn Dearg peaks, south-east of Ullapool, and another, not far from Forest Lodge, after a visit to Stob Ghabhar. Of course, this arrangement only applies to certain groups of hills—ideally, those approached by a long glen that has interesting possibilities at its farther end without getting on to the peaks. My wife keeps to marked tracks, knows when to turn back, and has a sufficiency of mountain experience that enables her to be sensible about these things.

Sometimes, on the few well-tracked Scottish mountains, my wife accompanies me to the tops, one such expedition in September 1973 being to Ben Nevis which she had not visited before. I wanted to go up the mountain again, visited several times, to pick up the two adjoining Munro tops of Carn Dearg (N.W.) and Carn Dearg (S.W.) which, according to my marked Munro's tables, I had not done. This shows how badly I was then smitten by the disease. While I was busy with the lower tops my wife went on to the summit where I later met her in a September snowstorm which turned, on our descent, into heavy rain. But the trip was splendidly rewarding, not only because of the tops collected in thick cloud, but for the sight from the summit of the Ben, of the mists clearing from the Carn Mor Dearg ridge and the tremendous north precipices of the highest mountain in Britain suddenly revealed, just below our feet. I had not visited these crags for years and the sight, with the patches of old snow still lingering in the gullies, stirred exciting memories.

We were caravanning on Loch Eil that year after several bed and breakfast holidays. Like many regular visitors to Scotland we have several favourite places where we have often stayed—one in Glencoe village, for instance, and others in Arran and the Cairngorms—and in recent years we have discovered several more. One particularly good find was at Ullapool where we booked in for bed and breakfast one night and stayed for ten days, dinner included, for a ridiculously small amount. Ullapool, and this comfortable house, proved a convenient centre for a great deal of fine mountain country. Ben More Assynt, with its long rocky ridge to the south, was collected on an extremely warm day. It seemed a long trudge up Glen Dubh from Inchnadamph, particularly as the neighbouring Munro of Conival had to be ascended first, but the Cambrian quartzite on top provided good going and the height gave welcome relief from the midges and assorted insect life that had plagued me in the glen. There were magnificent views from the summit ridge of many of the strange peaks of Torridon sandstone that skirt the coastline of Wester Ross, but the highlight of rather a tiring, lonely day was a dip in a rock-pool, sheltered by birches and lighted by the setting sun, and later, near a waterfall a mile from the loch, several cups of newly-brewed tea.

The highest mountain in Scotland north of the Garve to Ullapool road is Beinn Dearg, the red mountain, which I reached from the Inverlael Forest—traversed by car with the permission of a kindly Forestry Commission officer. The walk up the glen, under the spectacular northern crags of the mountain, up the zigzags and past a string of tiny lochans to the col, is delightful, and I found the mountain, although 3,547 feet in height, one of the easiest in the highlands. Coire Ghranda, ringed by savage cliffs with a beautiful tarn below, is a particularly impressive place, but the top of the mountain would be smooth enough in places for a cricket pitch. From the col two adjoining summits, each about a mile away, are worth collecting and are both Munros and I remember feeling so fit, after the easy ascent, that I ran nearly all the way up Meall nan Ceapraichean—the only time I can remember running up a mountain since my youth.

Facing the Beinn Dearg range across the Ullapool road are the Fannich Forest peaks with the highest, Sgurr Mor (3,637 feet), especially impressive as a steep, shapely summit dominating the country to the south of Braemore Forest. This was tackled from the main road, initially by the way of Allt a' Mhadaidt, which had to be forded at one place and, on the way back, proved an irritating obstacle at the end of a fairly hard day. My wife walked to the dark lochan underneath the northern cliffs on the mountain while I made straight up the steep slopes to the summit, and then south-east for 3 or 4 miles along the ridge. This is deer country which generally means that the going is tiring—trackless, the grass unkempt and not well cropped as on the sheep fells of Lakeland, and the slopes kicked about by sliding feet. Many of the best mountains in Scotland are under deer and you can quickly recognize them, even before you see the prints, for deer are not nearly so tidy on a mountain as sheep. The feral smell of deer, after they have passed over an area, is also quite distinctive. There are ten Munros and three Munro tops in the Fannichs and I collected half the total on this one day which proved very much harder than the Beinn Dearg round done two days earlier. The southern slopes of the Fannichs descending to the loch are smooth and gentle but to the north are fine cliffs and many wild corries, most of them with lochs and lochans, so that the ground is much more interesting but also more demanding. There was no time to include the western summits but I managed to fit in Beinn Liath Mhor Fannaich on the way back giving me a wonderful descent in the evening sunlight, with the insects whirring in the heather, the scent of bog myrtle in my nostrils, and the great bulk of the Beinn Dearg range reaching up, straight ahead, into the northern sky. And later, my long-suffering wife, back from her walk to the loch, was able to spot me coping with that irritating, winding burn, which, unless you are cleverer than I am, has to be crossed two or three times, and had the tea ready by the roadside—slightly spoiled, I seem to recall, by the rattle and smell of tar-spraying a mile or two above the Aultguish Inn.

One bright September day in 1970 Ivan Waller and I did the round of the ten 4,000-feet tops in the Cairngorms, starting from the car-park on the ski-road at the disgustingly early hour of half past seven. It took us 11 hours to complete the circuit in an anti-clockwise direction, including nearly 3½ hours, going pretty steady, to reach Braeriach, our first summit. The distances are long in the Cairngorms—the largest area of high ground in Britain and, in places, further away from habitation or help than anywhere else in the country. We passed the reindeer grazing among the heather and, on our first descent into the Lairig Ghru, came upon some youngsters on an adventure-course, washing in the burn, who offered us a welcome cup of tea—the only people we saw all day. From the top of Sron na Lairig on our way up to the first of Braeriach's four summits we looked down into the pass and saw the morning sunlight shining on the Pools of Dee, 2,000 feet below, and the river winding like a silver thread through the dark defile. Later, on the vast Braeriach plateau, we came upon the Wells of Dee where the river, 85 miles long and the fastest flowing river in Scotland, has its source—4,000 feet above sea-level. No other river in the country has such a source at such a height—a spring gushing out of the grass and mosses, with cushions of moss campion not far away, and great crags dropping down towards the glen. Over these crags plunges the infant Dee in a tumbling cascade into the corrie 500 feet below and at their foot lay a large patch of snow—one of the very few snow-fields in Britain that normally remain right through the year. And there was another larger snow-field just below the summit of Ben Macdhui. The ice-floes that may be seen in mid summer floating on the edge of Loch Coire an Lochain, the highest lochan or tarn in the British Isles, had disappeared, and the sun was sparkling on the beautiful green lochan caught in a hanging corrie just below the summit of Sgorr an Lochain Uaine (the Angel's Peak).

Lunch was taken perched on the summit rocks of Cairn Toul, perhaps the finest of the Cairngorm peaks, and forty minutes later we were fording the Dee, not far from the Corrour bothy. Since my feet, encased in an old but comfortable pair of boots, were wet through already, I plunged through the burn, but Ivan, with more thought for his footgear, waded painfully across in bare feet, his boots hung round his neck. The 2,400 feet of steep ascent by the Allt Clach nan Taillear (the Tailor's Burn) to the top of Ben Macdhui, the second highest mountain in Britain, was taken steadily, without a stop, but aided by dextrose tablets. Tradition has it that three tailors perished in the snow near this place on New Year's Eve. They had wagered they would dance a reel on the same night in Rothiemurchus and in Braemar but in crossing the Lairig Ghru succumbed to the elements. We avoided any misfortune and, after ticking off the Ben Macdhui summits, continued the walk over Cairn Lochan to Cairngorm on a perfect evening and then trotted down the eroded ski slopes to the car. The sun was sinking behind the gap in the hills through which we had passed ten hours earlier and shining on the waters of Loch Morlich, among the Scots firs. It had been a very good day.

Ivan and I have enjoyed several expeditions in the Scottish hills, including two successive days in the Mamores in the summer of 1973. There are sixteen 3,000-feet tops, including ten Munros, in the Mamore Forest south of Ben Nevis, and very tough people do them all in one day. Indeed, one determined young mountaineer, having done all sixteen, carried on along all the tops of the Grey Corries, the Aonachs, Carn Mor Dearg and Ben Nevis, a most remarkable performance. But Ivan and I, with ages totalling 128 years, thought we should reserve two days for the Mamores alone—and even then had to leave Am Bodach for another day. Starting from Polldubh in Glen Nevis we did the western hills on the first day, adding the eastern hills from Kinlochleven after rather a heavy night in our caravan near Loch Eil. We encountered some mist and rain on the tops and I distinguished myself by taking a wrong compass bearing on the first Munro which landed us on an unscheduled top 15 feet lower than the magic 3,000 feet contour. My companion took this philosophically enough, even thanking me for putting in an extra summit, although by mistake, but it is a sobering thought that comparatively few people visit the pleasantly rocky summit of Meall a Chaoruinn—one of the unfortunate results of over-pedantic Munro-bagging. One of the strange sights on this first day was of two specks—people, obviously—moving backwards and forwards, at great speed, over the rocky summit of Stob Ban. We exchanged many theories about what might be happening during the half-hour approach to the summit, from some sort of race to mystic rites, but the situation was finally explained by two photographers, hidden among the summit boulders, who said they'd been on the hill since early morning trying to get a particular shot but had been constantly thwarted by the weather. They were prepared, they said, to remain up there for several more hours, so we left them to it. I was never quite clear whether their rapid peregrinations had been brought about by dashes to likely vantage points, or merely an effort to keep warm.

We ended that day by the interesting passage of the Devil's Staircase on to Sgurr a' Mhaim—a welcome feature on a walk along smooth ridges—and the long descent of the north-west ridge to the glen and the car which we must have had in our sights for an hour. The second day's peak-bagging which included Binnein Mor, at 3,700 feet the highest of the Mamores, took us into interesting country with some especially fine views of the Glencoe hills. And the evening scene from the heights of the setting sun shining on the great fiord of Loch Linnhe as it reached out towards the sea was unforgettable. It was difficult to place the horizon for the golden loch seemed part of the sky until we saw, seemingly even higher in the heavens, the mountains of Ardgour.

But I am finding it difficult to compress forty years of adventuring in the Scottish hills into one chapter. Rereading my untidy typescript I am dismayed to find nothing about days on the Buachaille above Glencoe, nothing about scores of skiing days in the years before chairlifts and mountain roads, and little or nothing about the islands—except Skye. Foolishly, I have never kept a diary of my mountaineering for longer than a month or two so that many of the memories have fused together and a dozen days in, for example, Glencoe become a jumbled picture of steep rock in the morning sun, mint cake and chocolate on airy ledges, compass work on misty ridges, and skiing in the sunshine, high above the clouds. Several Munros have been picked up on skis including Glas Maol, Beinn Ghlas, some of the Tarmachans and tops near Lochnagar, and many others in snow. There was a heavy snowstorm during a lone ascent of Schiehallion and first step-cutting lessons for my son on Tom Buidhe, a perfect day with Robin on The Saddle when we had to rope a frightened tourist down the Forcan ridge and a long, lonely day on the tops above Kinlochhourn where I fell in a bog up to my waist and could not get away from the smell all day. Occasionally, of course, there were defeats and I especially remember an early family attack on Slioch which failed only a short distance from the summit. We were camping near Kinlochewe at the time and the downpour on the mountain must have been dispiriting for children; I know it was for me. Particularly wretched was the descent through the tallest and wettest bracken I have ever encountered, while the midges at our camp site were the most numerous and vicious I have ever known. Sodden through to the skin and practically eaten alive by black swarms that filled the tents, we finally abandoned our desperate attempts to prepare a meal and fled to the fleshpots of the hotel.

The Beinn Eighe range, in thick mist, provided good compass practice, for at the end of the day I had to strike a line to reach my wife, left some hours earlier collecting lochs from the Torridon road. Years later, the Stob Ghabhar tops from Inveroran made a wonderful day, excellently rounded off by an evening in one of the best Highland inns, but I thought Beinn Laoigh (popularly, Ben Lui) the same week rather a tiring expedition. I went up from the Dalmally road and first had to climb a thousand feet through newly planted conifers, with deep trenches in between, which makes particularly difficult going. Great areas of the Highlands are now being afforested, making access to the hills something of a problem in places, and completely altering the scenery. Beinn Voirlich from Lochearnhead proved a very easy mountain, but entertaining, because on the summit there was a man with a particularly high-powered telescope mounted on the triangulation column which provided close-up views over a considerable area of Scotland. Especially interesting was the view of the dam west of Ben Lawers about 15 miles away, which seemed so close that you could study the stonework in detail.

Although I first saw Ben Lomond more than forty years ago I have never been on the mountain—largely because I have always been on my way to what are, for me, more interesting areas. Besides, Loch Lomond has never breathed of the Highlands for me and I am always glad when I have got through Glen Falloch and reached the gateway at Crianlarich. But some day, perhaps on a weekend from the Lakes, I will have to have a look at the Ben and perhaps will be greatly surprised. The principal omissions in my Munro list, at the time of writing, are, however, the Ben Alder group and the Ladhar Bheinn peaks in Knoydart, between Loch Nevis and Loch Hourn. I am continually hearing and reading of the attractions of these two remote mountain areas and hope to be able to explore these areas before very long. It would be appropriate to end the collection—if I ever get that far, which I often doubt—with either one or the other of these wonderful districts.

The best mountain, somebody once wrote, is the one you are climbing, and although I don't agree with this it is probably true that more recent impressions are particularly persuasive. My favourite Scottish mountains are mostly in Skye, but of those on the mainland I would find it impossible to select the half-dozen that have most impressed me, although I dare say I could choose fifty. Certainly, I cannot think of any Scottish mountain that has not given me some pleasure, no matter what the conditions; no Scottish mountain to which I would not be glad to return. I am only grateful I had the good fortune to discover mountains in my youth and that I have had sufficiently good health to enjoy them for a lifetime. Away from the popular summits, Scottish mountains have a flavour that I don't experience anywhere else, even in the Alps—an atmosphere of legend, history, quietude and remoteness that, even in the twentieth century, the Highlands still retain. Often, the beauty has been breathtaking—half of Scotland seen at a glance from some rocky pinnacle high above a deserted glen, sunlit snows reaching down to shadowed crags, remote green lochans and white burns tumbling through wooded gorges, the northern hills rising like ancient obelisks from watery plains, the magic of dawn from hills on the edge of the sea with the horizon crowded with islands, and sunset on a quiet shore, with the loch a pool of flaming gold, the Scots firs black against the sky, and the high snows rimmed with fire. There are places beyond the Grey Corries and the Aonachs or in the purple hills around Loch Carron or above the western lochs reaching out to the Atlantic, with no sheep about and the burns stilled and not even a whisper of sound in the glen, where the silence and the great loneliness and the feeling of being so very far from anywhere, can be a moving experience—enough to bring a man to search his soul.

SPRING IN THE HIGHLANDS

The flaming glory of the broom lighted our way up through the Highlands to the snows, and new bursting life on the pines and firs in the great forests on the edge of the mountains told of summer almost at hand. But high up there were snowdrifts half a mile long, snow cornices up to 20 feet thick, and one day—200 yards away from where I was standing—a tremendous avalanche. I had spotted the track of an old avalanche and was keeping well to one side when suddenly there was a loud crash followed by a roar and, turning round, I saw several hundred tons of snow and rock cascading down the hillside. The remains of a snow-field perched above steeply sloping slabs had suddenly slid over the edge. Nothing could have survived the crashing torrent and the mangled remains of sheep at the foot of another avalanche track some distance away told of an earlier unseen tragedy of the mountains. But elsewhere life was going on undisturbed. The ptarmigans, not yet out of their winter plumage, rose croaking from the new green heather shoots and the blaeberry at the side of the snow-drifts as we skied past, the reindeer who live in these parts nosed about among the boulders, and now and then we spotted red deer bounding elegantly up the hillside. Only on the mountain-tops where the snow will linger for a long time yet is the summer still far away; in the valleys it has arrived. Too early yet for the full glory of the heather but the broom, the new green on the pines and the spruce, the dainty tracery of the birch, and the lush carpet of herbs and fronds, sprouting through the pine needles, are there in compensation. And little green lochans sparkle in the evening sunlight and mirror the blue shapes of the snow-patterned hills.

Index